THE AGENCY
BUILD
GROW
REPEAT

Fiftyfive Books

© Luca Senatore 2019

ISBN 978-1-9160151-0-4

Fiftyfive
Books
Publishing

FIFTYFIVE BOOKS

THE AGENCY BUILD GROW REPEAT

How To Build a Remarkable Digital Agency Business
That Wins and Keeps Clients

LUCA SENATORE

CONTENTS

INTRODUCTION

This book is for agency people: founders, CEOs, MDs, employees, entrepreneurs and anyone else involved in the agency world. I'm talking about design, SEO, PPC, marketing, CRO, development, analytics, branding, PR, recruitment, and everything in between.

Over the past 12 months, I have been invited by Google to speak to the top three percent of agencies in the EMEA region about how we run a successful digital agency and deliver the best performance for our clients. I have spoken at Google in London, Milan, and Berlin in front of some of the best agencies in the world. When they asked me the question: "what do you think is the one thing that every agency can do to be better, more successful and more profitable?" my answer has always been the same. And to this day, I stand by it strongly.

My answer is that if every single agency did a better job, if every agency did a perfect job for their clients and delivered a remarkable experience, then every single agency would be more successful and more profitable. The truth is that there is still a huge number of potential advertisers who are sceptical of working with agencies. There is still a large number of potential clients who, when you walk in and tell them that you are from an agency, act as if you are telling them you're the Antichrist, running to grab their crosses. Yet these people, who perhaps chose to manage their digital marketing in-house, are our potential customers. They could be in the market for agencies, if agencies had a better reputation.

In 2013 we built Genie Goals, a digital marketing agency that specialises in paid channels and works exclusively with retail brands. Our goal was to revolutionise digital marketing for retail brands but also to positively impact the whole industry and improve the reputation of agencies. As part of our sales process (there's a lot more on this in the chapter THE SELLING) we audit an incredible number of accounts. Often these accounts are in terrible shape, either because there was clearly a lack of talent and expertise within the team at the agency that managed the account, or because there was a lack of resources, and too little time was assigned to the account.

On one hand, that makes our sales process very easy; it's a no-brainer for the client to switch agency and come to us, especially when we show them what we would do, why, and what results the changes would be likely to produce.

On the other hand, it always makes me sad because I know that accounts in such terrible shape and teams that deliver such bad performance dent the advertiser's trust and confidence in agencies. How many times does an advertiser need to be burned before they lose total confidence in the whole industry and decide to bring the activity in-house? Or even worse, decide that a particular channel 'doesn't work'?

We have managed to persuade clients who had lost all confidence in PPC or social media to give it another try and helped them see that these could in fact be effective channels for their business. After a few weeks of high-quality work, these channels turned out to perform, and within a few months to a couple of years, they had become the biggest source of revenue and new customers for these clients.

But how many 'unpersuadable' customers are there for each one that we win? If every single agency did an incredible job, if they delivered on their promised performance, then the reputation of the industry in general would be better and we'd all win – you, us, everybody. Higher confidence in the industry = higher demand. Higher demand = more business.

That's exactly why I wrote this book. I want to share the things that we have learned, that we have done and are doing which make us good. The stuff that makes us worthy of being invited by Google to speak to the top three percent of agencies in the EMEA region. The stuff that makes us lose very few clients and that made us grow as much and as fast as we did.

I will also share all the things that I know we're not doing yet, the things that we are aspiring to do, which will make us even better. I want to share the methodologies. I want to share the theory, the practice, the case studies, the examples, the strategies, and the techniques that make our agency a good agency – and those that will make our agency even better once we adopt them.

In this book, I've included everything from working out your mission and your big WHY to recruitment, goal setting, objectives and key results (OKRs), selling, marketing, executing, contracts, relationship management, and whatever else you need to know to build a new agency, or grow your existing one and take it to the next level. I have left nothing out, no secrets unshared. I have also interviewed brands for their take on what they want from, like or dislike about agencies. I have interviewed people from the industry for their take on it. I have interviewed other large agencies and I've included all the elements that will help you build and grow your super agency, the agency of the future.

I really hope this book will bring value and that it helps you build or grow a better agency – a solid business delivering quality work you and your teams can be proud of. I want you to build an incubator of happiness, creating, in the words of my good friend Geoff Griffiths, former professional rugby player and MD of Builtvisible, "meaningful experience for your team and for your customers". I've included everything I know to help you do that. But you have to do your part for this to work. You have to act. One of the key elements of success, the single factor that will allow you to grow, and be proud of your work, is action. You can read this book hundreds of times, word by word, letter by letter, but if you don't implement anything, nothing will ever change. Inspiration is the spark that starts the engine, but action is the gas that keeps it running. No action, no motion; no motion, no growth.

My biggest piece of advice is to read this book once, and then read it again as if you're reading a manual or a how-to book. That way, you'll be able to implement the ideas you find useful. When you find something that you want to – and can – implement immediately, stop reading. Make a note of the action you want to take and then go on to finish the chapter. As soon as you complete each chapter, take action, implement what you can which is relevant to that chapter and build a roadmap. Once you have set the machine in motion, once the projects or tasks are being actioned, go back to reading the next chapter.

Caution: In the first half of the book, I talk about things I've done well, things that worked, the victories. Later I talk about the failures, the mistakes, the vulnerability that inevitably anyone building anything will encounter. Don't let the early chapters fool you into thinking I think I know it all; I don't. Don't think I am super-human; I am absolutely not, and I know it. I mention my achievements early on because they frame the book the way it needs to be framed. There will be plenty to discover about me stumbling, failing and falling, just keep reading.

It is my sincere hope that you'll build a remarkable business, one that makes you proud, makes you happy and makes you better at what you do.

We will keep this book alive. Things change, especially now. Change happens quickly, and change is dramatic, so we need to keep things relevant. To do that, I have created a live version of this book at lucasenatore.co.uk/theagency. Be sure to visit the site for additional resources, tools, and updates on the content of this book.

Join these two groups. I created these to provide additional help and resources to grow your agency business:

- Facebook: goo.gl/QLfvHh

- Linkedin: goo.gl/b94sif

Connect with me: @lucasenatore

Good luck and enjoy the reading.

SECTION ONE: BUILD

This section is about creating YOUR AGENCY. That doesn't mean that it's only for those who are starting out or thinking of starting out. Even businesses that have been established for years might, and most probably at some point will, need to *re*create themselves – to create something new, to create something different. This section touches on certain elements of creating your agency, your business and your next thing. And when you create something, it's far more than the word may suggest. Creating something in business means you're giving something life; you're giving life to something that you hope to see grow and succeed. You're bringing something to life that wasn't there before and that wants to become something remarkable.

Much like any new life, whatever you choose to create deserves respect, and it deserves your love and attention. I see so many micro businesses starting and so many established businesses changing without really giving the creation or the change much respect. Even moving office is part of the process of creating, because you're creating a new environment where your people will work, and your customers will visit you. When you move office, throw an office party, send out an announcement. Celebrate the birth of your new thing.

When we create something, we must have a mission for it. That mission has to be bigger than us and bigger than money and profits, as we argue in the next chapter, THE WHY. You need to be fixated on your goal and where you want to go, but you must also be flexible as to how you're going to get there.

The moment you become too fixated and obsessed on the road itself, the destination may become out of reach. If roadworks and accidents or anything else happens on the road to your destination, you might get stuck. You need to be prepared, flexible and adaptable, so that you can change the route and still get to your destination. Some routes to your destination will be longer, some shorter; some routes will be smoother and some rougher. It doesn't matter if you take longer, it doesn't matter if the journey is harder. As long as you are obsessed about what you want to achieve and flexible about how you get there, then you will give yourself the best chances of success.

This section is all about creating, reinventing, growing. When you grow you are creating – you're creating *more* of something. And even then, it's unlikely that you'll create more of the same; in growing, you want new elements and new dynamics, new branches, new services, new channels, new people, new departments. That's all part of creating.

This is what we mean by create. In the chapters that follow you'll find all the elements we have considered and used when creating, when growing. And we're still going through the process, I doubt we will ever stop (the moment we stop, I think I'll probably be very bored and start looking for something else). This is not always an iterative process, it's a never-ending process – you're always creating. I'm creating right now, and you are creating right now – in your mind you have ideas and thoughts, and plans might be taking shape.

So give that creation the respect it deserves by planning it, putting action behind it and treating it like a new thing that has come to life.

Next, you'll be introduced to THE WHY. It is absolutely vital that we have a strong WHY, and you'll learn how you can build a strong WHY. Then comes THE PEOPLE – discover how you can find, train and keep your best team members. THE MARKETING and THE SALES follow: how do we put our business in front of the people that want to buy? How do we sell? Finally, you'll be introduced to THE COMMUNICATION, and learn how to talk to your teams and customers and how it's not only what you say but how you say it that makes a massive difference. All these elements and much more will help you create, recreate and grow THE AGENCY OF THE FUTURE. Enjoy.

THE WHY

I have vague memories of my father driving expensive cars and somehow had the sense that we had a luxurious lifestyle. I also have some memories of being scared of my dad, that I didn't like him, and that the only emotion I had toward him was fear. I honestly don't remember feeling anything else about him. But I don't really recall much else about that time, nothing specific at least. My parents split up when I was very young, probably about five, I can't be sure. My mum and I were left with nothing, from one day to the next. We didn't have any money, debt piled up quickly, and things were difficult. At times we were living from meal to meal.

The real challenge, I now know, wasn't so much the 'what', it wasn't the fact that we were poor and that my mum was a single mum. It was mainly challenging because we were different. We were different from most other people around us – back then in Italy, it wasn't common for people to divorce. Where I come from, Valmadrera, a pretty small village near Lecco on Lake Como, everyone around me had more money than we did – that didn't take much – and everyone I knew had a father and some sort of, at least apparent, stability. I know now that this does not mean they were happier than us; I later understood what real happiness is and I learnt that happiness and normality are not the same thing, and that normality certainly doesn't guarantee happiness.

Because of the lack of stability and structured education, as well as not having a role model, I had absolutely no idea as to what I wanted to do with my life when I grew up – no sense of direction or example to follow. I didn't even know what I could aspire to. My future didn't look the brightest, and this lack of stability and role model meant my confidence was low. In my undeveloped mind, the fact that we were so different meant I had to find different tools to most of my peers. The skills and stories you learn by doing chores for your father as he does DIY, I had to learn somewhere else. The sense of union and family – group dynamics, including negotiating, compromising and co-living – you learn when you have a busy household, I had to learn somewhere else.

So I learnt pretty quickly, before the topic of 'fake it until you make it' became mainstream, that I had to pick some role models, some examples to follow. The good thing about my father leaving and my not being able to find a role model in my family was that I could choose whomever I wanted to be a role model. I had no limits. I just needed to pick someone I liked and could have close to me. I picked Bruce Lee as my main role model, plus a few other characters from movies I liked: Superman, Rocky and various others who I emulated depending on the situation.

I would walk around literally pretending I was them. I would think what I thought they would think. I would move the way I thought they'd move. The result was that I appeared way more confident than I actually was. So I went about it differently, taking on the part of one of my role models: the classic outcast that doesn't fit in and will one day emerge in victory, surprising everyone. I became quite a rebel, and the place where this showed the most was, of course, school.

I remember one day in particular, the last day of the last year at secondary school. All my friends were going to high school after that year. I had a job lined up as we couldn't afford for me to study. We were in the school gymnasium where all the final year classes came together for their last goodbyes. Being the very last day of the very last year in that school, everyone was celebrating, playing around and saying their goodbyes to teachers and fellow students. A few were even doing cartwheels and gymnastics moves – I was one of them.

Ms Gandini, our English language teacher, came over, very angry about what we were doing. She decided to take me, just me, and send me to the Head's office. During the past year, Ms Gandini had never marked my work but always classified it as "'ungradable", equivalent to a U, apart from once when I manage to get a "severely insufficient", equivalent to an F.

We got to the Head's office, but the Head was out for a few hours. Ms Gandini told me to wait there and she left. After 20 or 30 minutes she came back to check if the Head had returned, but he hadn't. She then looked at me and said: "okay, if you apologise, I'll let you off the hook." But I was a rebel, and I knew I was right when I contested being the only one in trouble when several students had been doing the same thing (which, incidentally, wasn't all that inappropriate since we were in a gymnasium). So I refused to apologise; I felt I had nothing to apologise for.

She didn't like that at all and stormed out, leaving me to wait in the Head's office. Half an hour later she returned to find the Head was still not back. She offered the deal again, and I rejected it again – politely, but with an obvious smirk. She lost it. She started screaming at me that she'd make sure I'd never be allowed in any Italian school ever again, that I was going nowhere in life and that I would be a failure.

What do these stories have to do with growing an agency, or any business? I hear you ask. They are important. These stories form part of my WHY. Part of who I am. They form some of my deepest values. These stories are the moulds of some of my strongest WHYs and some of my most important goals.

Because of the emotionally charged events with Ms Gandini – not only the one I just described, but many throughout the year – I was absolutely determined to learn English. And I was absolutely going to be a success. Ms Gandini's words echoed so freaking loudly in my head for so many years that I couldn't ignore them. Those experiences touched me so deeply that there was no way I was going to let Ms Gandini be right about me. Didn't she know? I was Bruce Lee, Superman, Knight Rider and Rocky, all in the body of one slightly overweight lazy-eyed boy. I was going to make it, one way or another.

I didn't have a father I could play with and learn from and I wasn't able to do things other kids were able to; the feeling of being 'less than' stuck to me like a wetsuit and a voice shouted in my head that I was never going to be successful, never going to have a family. I had two choices then: I could either believe and accept these thoughts or use them and change my story, affect my destiny. They were my WHY for breaking the mould, my WHY for changing my life in the way I wanted rather than being affected *by* life. They were my WHY for not being what I was told I was going to be, and there was no stopping me – there was no way in hell I was going to quit. Rocky never quits.

Many things have happened since then. I have literally transformed myself and managed to craft a life I am proud of. Have I 'made it'? Hell no! There's still tonnes of stuff I want to do, loads of things I need to improve on and change. I absolutely suck at many things (you'll find plenty of specific examples later on in the book). But I have also achieved a lot. Has all that I have achieved been a product of my childhood events? Probably not. There have been many other significant events in my life that positively affected my future. Loads of inspirational events and people came into my life and inspired me to do more, do better and be better, for me and for the world. Ms Campagni, for example, my literature teacher who always believed in me. And Amos and Omar Bresciani, the owners of the factory I worked at when I was 15, bending, welding and cutting metal for the building trade – they taught me a lot.

In the years since leaving school, I have gone from being allergic to studying to be a learning junkie. I am now 42 and I have focused on learning for the last 17 years; I'm still going strong, I'll never stop. First I had to master the English language, and then I dove into an array of subjects, including various forms of marketing, psychology, leadership, business and more. I listen to a stupid number of audiobooks and audio courses and push myself to be a better person every day. Better to my family – trying to not be a dick when challenges get in the way, trying to not take my family for granted. Better to others – trying to really listen, to be more empathetic and helpful. Better to the world – trying to do more of the right things and less of the things that hurt our planet. I fail at all of this, regularly, but I keep trying.

My journey started when it was all about me, all about changing things I wanted to change, all about not being what I was afraid of becoming, being different from who I was in the past and different from my father. It was very self-centred. Today it's more about others, about touching as many people as possible in a positive way.

So it wasn't all because of Ms Gandini or my father or my childhood circumstances, but these things have been a massive driver of that initial spark. And whilst I don't thank my father or Ms Gandini for this, as they had zero idea about the effect they would have, I am extremely grateful to the universe and

15

the circumstances that caused these events, because they have given me a strong WHY, just like other events and people have done in other areas of my life.

I honestly don't think I would have achieved much had I not understood the vital importance of giving myself powerful reasons to do what I want to do – the importance of building strong WHYs. When you have a strong WHY, you build much stronger resistance to adversity, you're more resilient, you take things more to heart, you don't quit, and you become unstoppable. When you have a strong WHY, you build strong answers to questions that will form the culture in your business, the ethos, the energy and the stuff that your employees and clients will love you for. When you have a strong WHY, your mission is clear, unmovable and unshakable because they are founded on values that are super important to you. This is true for most things in life, and it's certainly vital when building a business.

My dear friend, and MD of Genie Ventures, Ciaron Dunne is one of the most successful people I know, and he has great ethos and values. He's totally loved and admired by everyone in the company, including me. When talking about his WHY, he said:

"We wanted to create a place of work where people want to go, where people are happy and enjoy spending time in."

If you build a strong WHY, then you won't find yourself torn trying to make important decisions – they come easily.

For me, having strong WHYs meant developing into a very different person to the projected version of my younger self. I became a me who has a strong sense of stability, with my wife of 12 years, our kids, my profession, finances and all the things I wanted but couldn't feel stable about. The power of WHY is relevant in everything I do.

As a side project, at the end of 2017, I decided to open a new Brazilian Jiu Jitsu (BJJ) academy in Cambridge. Of all the martial arts gyms around, only 1 percent or less manage to turn a healthy profit. And that is 1 percent of those that manage to stay open past the first year. It's safe to say that my WHY was not money.

I have a black belt in Karate and Kickboxing, and yet I decided to open an academy for a martial art in which I had a white belt. A friend, with a purple belt, was going to teach the classes once I set up the academy and I was going to market the business. The unit I had found was next door to a Karate school, which had been going for 25 years. A few doors down to the right there was a fitness gym and a few doors down to the left a boxing gym.

Our ambition was to be a children and beginners academy. I personally love BJJ and feel it's the most effective and interesting form of martial arts. I wanted to train in it and I wanted my children to train in it. The problem was that there was nowhere with good enough standards for kids and adults alike to train in a safe, clean and inspiring environment. The nearby children's martial arts gyms seemed to be motivated primarily by profit, and I saw kids kept motivated by the idea of grading and chasing belts. They also charged amounts that only a few families could afford to pay.

I wanted to convince adults, those who felt that learning new things was not possible – I wanted them to believe that they could do stuff they thought they couldn't. I wanted children, irrespective of gender, whether they have both parents or only one, or none, and irrespective of their financial situation, to not only *know* but truly *feel* that sense of conviction that they are amazing, that they are worthy of all the good things they want to go after, that they must be confident, kind and resilient.

The purpose of the academy wasn't to create a business, but rather to create a remarkable experience for all who came into contact with it. These elements formed a massively strong WHY, and because of my strong WHY, it was always easy to say "no" to ideas that might have given us extra cash in the short term but would probably have killed our interest in the long term. Decisions like introducing different disciplines we didn't love just for the sake of attracting more students, compromising on customer experience (through an app, website, marketing, payment processing, etc.) to decrease costs, and building an overly easy curriculum to keep people interested.

Because of my strong WHY it was easier to push through adversity. The cause was bigger than me and it was worth persevering for. When the electrician sent me a quote that was five times higher than expected because he found unexpected problems with the wiring, it was easy to say "go ahead". When the structural engineers took longer than originally planned to visit the site, it was easy to find the time to chase them. When it came down to ordering the equipment, it was easy to choose the absolute best stuff. The end result was the best equipped, the best looking and the best branded academy around.

After a few months, we made contact with two of the best BJJ practitioners in the world, multi-time world champion black belts who were relocating from the USA. They eventually became good friends and partners to whom I sold most of the business at cost. I'm still involved – I have 15 percent of the business and Ciaron has 10 percent. After less than a year from the opening day, we have more than 120 students and are one of the most successful and admired academies in the country. It's called Rolling Dojo, check it out if you are ever in Cambridge in the UK.

At Genie Goals, our WHYs are:

1. To truly revolutionise the digital marketing industry, one retail brand at a time.

2. To create the best possible environment one might want to be in. We want to surround ourselves with people we admire, who inspire us and who we like spending time with.

These are way bigger WHYs than making a profit, way bigger than any of us as individuals and way bigger than any material success we can think of. These strong WHYs allow us to make decisions prioritising our people and our work before our profit. Don't get me wrong, profit is important, it enables businesses and people to do the good things they do. Profit is indeed a very important thing, just not a good motivator.

Building something remarkable isn't easy; you will find challenges and obstacles that will set you back, keep you up and night and make you wonder what you're doing all of that for. That's when you need a big, strong and powerful WHY. People who win are often not those with the better ideas, not those with more resources and not those with the better talent. People who win are those who don't quit, those who keep going when the going gets tough. And the only force that can keep us going when the going gets really fucking tough is having strong reasons to keep going: strong WHYs.

So make sure you have a robust WHY for your agency; if you do it just for the money, just for the success or the numbers, you are very likely to fail. It's way too easy at the first sign of adversity to adjust your expectations and compromise on your materialistic goals – "I don't need to make a million", "if we are not the biggest in the country it doesn't matter" and so on. If you have a stronger WHY that you are connected to at a deep emotional level, that is connected to your core values, then you are way less likely to back down; today's pain is justified because your goals are bigger than money, bigger than numbers and bigger than you. When your goals are connected to a strong, deep-rooted WHY, then they are worth fighting for. When that happens, you will become a very dangerous competitor for anyone in your space. The Rocky of your industry.

So before you lose yourself in the numbers, before you worry about anything else, worry about figuring out your WHY. I promise you will not regret it.

Actions

- Take some time out to think of your WHY, for yourself as an individual and for your business. Do this whether you own the business or work in it as an employee.

- Once you've given this some thought, write it down and make it known – own it.

THE
'DO WHAT YOU LOVE'
ARGUMENT

Take a moment to think about the things that you would like to do in life. Not just to do with work, but the things that you would like to do in general. Smaller things, not just the big things. Things like taking your partner to dinner, going to the theatre. Things like spending one-to-one time with each of your children. Watching that movie you wanted to watch, reading that book, perhaps skydiving. Whatever you have in mind that you would like to do at some point in the future, particularly the things you'd like to do soon but that keep taking a backseat and getting postponed to 'next week' or 'next month'.

Think of the one-off things that you would like to do, things that perhaps you should be able to do one of each month – one month you skydive, the next month you commit to reading that book, and so on. Also think about the things you would like to do every month, like taking your family to dinner, watching at least one good movie or documentary, taking one full day undisturbed and undistracted to spend time with your family. These things are relatively small – important, indeed, but part of normal life. You want to do them, but you know you won't be able to every month. You just accept it.

Take a moment to think about that, because I think you might find what follows profound. I started thinking of the things that I wanted to do each month, exactly the things I've just mentioned: spending one-to-one time with each of my children, taking them to the movies, taking my wife to a new place for dinner and giving us my truly undivided attention, starting this book and so on. Then I realized that several months had gone by without me having been able to do those things regularly; I realized that maybe I was only doing them every other month, or every three months, and that some of the stuff I wanted to do regularly hadn't happened at all.

Then something occurred to me. I think I was at a conference and someone mentioned a fact that has not only stuck with me but has profoundly affected how I prioritise. At my age, 42, if I am to live past 80 (which I assume I will) I have less than 500 months to live. Fuck! 500 months! 500 isn't a big number at all. And all of a sudden, my perspective changed dramatically. Very dramatically.

I started thinking in weeks, and even days, which is why, for me, only setting large long-term goals doesn't work. It's okay to have those, but it's vital that I have daily goals that I want to accomplish, not just to do with work but for life in the wider sense – work, sport, relationships and everyday things. I realised that 'everyday things' are seldom done every day, and those 'at least once a month' things are sometimes never done at all. With 500 months left to live, if I postpone my 'once a month' things just once, I might only have 250 opportunities to do the stuff I love. Screw that.

If you think of the things you want and need to do in this way when planning your business or work, it becomes even more important to choose something you truly love. It becomes really important to do the stuff you have great passion for.

But that sparks another dilemma. Many motivational speakers will tell you that you just need to find something you love doing and do that. But it isn't quite that simple, not quite so easy. It raises a fundamental question, a big one: *what is it that you love?*

How on earth are you supposed to figure that out if you don't have any clear ideas? It isn't as easy as just thinking about it for five minutes and realizing "Oh yes, I love that thing, so I'm gonna do that." Coming up with something we really love can be a massive challenge that many never overcome. We may love something today, this year even, but we might not love it quite as much tomorrow or next month, or next year. So to ask ourselves today "What is it that I would love to do every single day of my life, for the rest of my life?" is a bit like asking a 15-year-old what they want to do when they grow up.

We know this doesn't work, because we can see that the majority of people who studied at university end up switching careers: according to a survey of 2,000 graduates carried out by the New College of the Humanities, 96 percent of people switch careers by the age of 24. This isn't the end of the world for students; the biggest value that studying brings isn't the knowledge of the subjects studied, as this changes and evolves anyway. The biggest skill that studying provides is the skill of learning. This is fortunate because if students had to sign a contract that committed them to work in the field they studied, we'd have a very large number of extremely unhappy members of society.

The point here is that it's not easy to find something you love; it's not easy when you're young and it doesn't get any easier as you get older. It's not easy to find something you think you're going to love for the rest of your life and just do that.

What is much easier, much more attainable, reliable and likely to survive the test of time, is to identify the values that are important to you, your core values. To find the principles and concepts that you love and that can form part of your non-negotiables. To find things that you can love every day in the context of what you do.

For example, I have immense passion for personal development and seeing other people inspired to be better because I have two core beliefs:

- Happiness is provided by the sense of progression and not status. An accomplished, healthy and wealthy individual might feel less happy than a person who's in difficult circumstances if the former is 'static' and the latter is progressing.

- Everyone on earth can progress, everyone can be better.

I feel it's important that I back up these beliefs. Perhaps the latter doesn't need much backing up, since I think we can all agree that the vast majority of people can get better at something – we can all set goals and progress. The former, however, might or might not be so easy to accept.

Research on goal pursuit and well-being suggests there is a cycle between progression and emotional well-being.[1] In a book chapter on the topic, German psychologist Prof Dr Bettina S. Wiese illustrates the cycle between progression and emotional well-being (which she refers to as subjective well-being, or SWB):

---

1 (Wiese, B. S. (2007). Successful pursuit of personal goals and subjective well-being. In B. R. Little, K. Salmela-Aro, & S. D. Phillips (Eds.), Personal project pursuit: Goals, action, and human flourishing (pp. 301-328). Mahwah, NJ, US: Lawrence Erlbaum Associates Publishers).

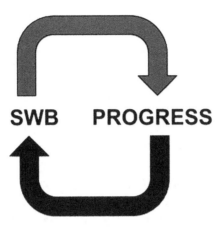

Wiese's research shows that as we make progress on our goals, our SWB increases: we feel happier. Feeling these positive emotions, she suggests, motivates us to pursue the goal even more. The research also concludes that the more difficult the goal we go after and achieve, the higher the SWB gets. So in simple terms:

Progress = Happiness. Happiness = Progress

I have great passion for inspiring others, especially younger people, to do better. I don't believe that I am, as a whole, better than anyone else. I might be better at something; others might be better at a different thing. When I see an individual who is better than me at something I want to improve on, I get inspired to learn from them and get better. That's why this book exists. This book doesn't exist to help you make all the money you want, it wasn't created for that. Sure, that may be a welcome side-effect, and if it happens, I'll be even more pleased. This book was created to inspire you. This book was created to make you better, in a way. Not because I am better than you; whether you are ahead of me or behind me is irrelevant. If I can add even one percent to where you are and what you do, then you will be better than you were.

This is why we should always be open to learning from anybody in the world, irrespective of where they are, how young they are, when they joined the company, or what they have achieved. Even if they are way, way, way behind you, they might have something to offer; in fact, I think they most probably would. And if you take that one percent, five percent, ten percent, whatever it is that they have to offer, then you become a better version of you. That is one of the reasons why this book exists: to inspire you, to help you be a better you.

A decade ago, the twenty-something-year-old intern would walk into the boardroom to bring the coffees. Today, the twenty-something-year-old intern walks in and tells everyone how to grow their brand online. If you refuse to be humble and ready to learn from anyone, you might never recover from the shock you'll get when you realise what you've missed out on. This is true in any situation, in business and life in general. I learn from my ten-year-old every day.

If I adopted a more traditional way of thinking, the one promoted by most motivational speakers and motivational theories, then I might be quite stuck right now. My options would be to quit what I am doing, quit my agency, maybe even quit writing this book to do what I love, which is to touch many people on a personal level. If I did that, I might become a full-time motivational speaker, writing about motivation and inspiration, publishing self-development books, doing seminars, and sharing videos and content all about that. Ironically, if I did that, I would probably not be able to touch as many people as I do now. It would be obvious that that's why I was there; the people who are resistant to personal development, not ready to embrace it in that way or simply unaware that they need it wouldn't access my content because it would be labelled personal development and therefore raise all the common presumptions.

Instead, I've chosen to use my passion, which is to inspire and help people be better, in everything that I do. If my job was that of collecting rubbish in the morning from residential homes, I would do the same. If I was a builder, I would do the same. If I was a lawyer, or a painter, or a singer, I would do the same. My job is to run a digital agency, so I'm doing it here. And I can do it by implementing either formal or informal, overt or covert, ways of inspiring my team, my staff, my colleagues, my clients, my customers, my audience, the people at conferences I speak at, my peers, everyone. I get to enjoy every single mile of the most scenic route I can take on my journey, irrespective of what I am driving – I focus on the outside.

So instead of trying to understand what you love doing and do that in your work, seek to understand what's important to you as a person and inject that into whatever you do.

Before you allow your pessimistic monkey (we all have one) to sabotage you, yes you can do this in any job and with any passion. If your passion is painting or being artistic, for example, but you find yourself in a job that doesn't lend itself to that, maybe you're a lawyer or the CEO of an analytics agency, there are many ways in which you can nurture your passion and use it in what you do.

Let's imagine I was the lawyer with a passion for drawing. I could create an artistic infographic about the branch of law I'm in. I'd use my artistic passion and skills to draw that infographic and move away from the traditional way of presenting legal information as well as from the traditional style of infographics. Or maybe my passion is singing; I could launch the singing lawyer podcast, all about legal issues, in harmony.

I am writing this section of the book on the move – I'm speaking into a voice recorder and thinking on the spot, so this might be a wild example. But my message is simple: if I can think of an example like this on the spot, I am confident that you, with your great passion, can come up with some decent ideas for applying what you love in your field.

LearnVest, a financial planning organisation, turned the financial planning industry on its head by creating a membership-based business that provides straightforward, understandable advice to people who are not clear on what to do to secure their financial future (most people). As well as providing advice, LearnVest also sells personal finance software.

CEO and Founder Alexa von Tobel had a strong WHY: she was just 14 when her father passed away unexpectedly, leaving Alexa and her mother to manage the family's finances, which had always been Alexa's father's job. Alexa and her mother experienced first-hand what it was like to lack stability and easy-to-understand information. As a result, Alexa became very determined to understand finance and help others plan for their future.

She went on to fund LearnVest in her mid-twenties when, after asking hundreds of people – young, old, rich or not – she discovered that no one knew how to even start planning for their future. She created a tool that simplifies financial planning and investing. Within three years, LearnVest was offering support to millions of people, and in 2015 Alexa sold the company, reportedly for about $250 million.

As well as having a strong WHY, Alexa was able to create a phenomenal and exciting business in an industry that she

28

found, in her words, boring. She introduced plain-English advice, which some finance veterans criticised her for, technology and innovation to help people feel stable when life brings potentially stability-reducing circumstances.

There are many opportunities to inject your passion into what you do. If you have a JOB (just over broke), you might be convincing yourself that your passion cannot be translated into something that you can do daily and profit from. I think that's really sad. I truly believe that every single person on the planet has something special to offer; but we know that we can only add true value when we're in a state of excitement and passion. Sure, choose to do something that you love, but if you're not in love with the technicalities and strict definition of what you do, then spice it up. Change it up a bit, inject your passion into what you do. You have no limits, I promise.

I have retired now from high-level martial arts, but I have competed in mixed martial arts (MMA, sometimes known as cage fighting). At the same time, I am leading a digital marketing agency and speaking at events. I need to interact with my staff and clients face-to-face. Obviously, when you do something like mixed martial arts, you might end up going to work with bruises on your face, or limping; although that hasn't really happened to me yet, there's always a chance I'll turn up with a big black eye.

How do I deal with that? I've made being a mixed martial arts athlete part of my brand. We worked on this at the agency: MMA was all over my LinkedIn profile and all over my Facebook profile; we published more than one blog post on the agency website about it and generally made it very much part of my brand.

The idea behind this is that you can turn that different side of you into something that can fit into your business or your job

– something quirky about you then becomes not only accepted but also a good talking point. This gives you a license to write about what you love even in a totally different environment. You could use your passion as a metaphor, drawing the attention of the reader to the overlapping commonalities between your passion and your work – in my case, high-impact competitive sport and business. Doing this allows me to talk about productivity and how I find ways to train so hard, whilst also running the agency, about courage, competitiveness, dealing with failure and hundreds of other business-related topics.

You see where I'm going with this. Making my passion part of my personal brand gives me more licence to use it in my business. It's open to my staff, it's open to my clients, it's open to everyone. This means that not only do they accept it when I come to work with a mark on my face, but they also they embrace that part of my identity; I've been introduced more than once as the MMA athlete who speaks to professional audiences on behalf of global organisations.

What this comes down to is that we really don't have much time. If you're around 40, you probably have about 500 months to do the stuff you want to do. When you realise this, you also realise that postponing things isn't a great idea. What are you going to do with your 500 months? What are you going to do every month? Every day? Whatever you do, you owe it to yourself, and to the world, to do it with passion and love.

Actions

- What are the things you really want to do but you don't have time for? Can you make these part of your professional profile?

- What are the things you absolutely want to do every week,

or even every day? Going to the gym, writing, learning UX, data analysis, having lunch with your partner? Make these part of your non-negotiables. Put the time in the calendar.

- Quit or delegate all the things you hate doing. You're probably not doing them very well anyway. Where possible, give these tasks to someone else and get on with the work that matters to you.

THE WHAT

What do you do? If you have your big WHY, now you need your big WHAT. I know that most of you reading this probably feel there are tens of elements about your agency that are important to include in your WHAT. But don't. There's time for this later. The *big* WHAT is a laser-focused spotlight on what you want to be known for. The features come later, the other services come later, the stuff you can upsell, cross-sell and diversify with come later. The big WHAT is the thing that makes you remarkably different, the thing people will remember you for. It's the difference between saying: "we do digital marketing" and "we exponentially grow performance through digital marketing for clients in travel and finance. If we don't think we can grow revenue, we won't take on the client".

I think that when you start a new venture in an existing market, your WHAT always comes down to a few key questions:

1. What's the proposition? What do you do?
2. What's different?
3. What's remarkable?
4. What problem do you solve?

If you cannot explain these four points succinctly and easily in less than one minute, then you've got more work to do. Work on your 'elevator pitch': could you pitch your proposition to possible investors or clients in an elevator?

It's important to be clear in your language. My personal view is that if you can't pitch it to your grandmother, you are likely drowning in tech speak. Think Apple, think Facebook, think major utilitarian technology that becomes part of the fabric of life, and simplify the proposition and how you talk about it.

Having total clarity about what you do, knowing what's different about your proposition compared to other solutions offered in the marketplace and knowing what important problem you are solving are among the most important elements that will enable you to win and stay on top. This level of awareness allows you to:

- Target the best segment within your target market – the 20 percent of people you're likely to create the best results for and who are likely to produce 80 percent of the results for you.

- Hire the right talent with attributes and passion for your vision and the problem you're solving.

- Build attractive a compelling sales and marketing assets like a website and pitching decks.

- Build a pricing structure based on the value you bring through your different USPs.

This doesn't just apply for startups and small agencies, it goes for anyone, irrespective of how long you have been in business. It is important to stop every so often and remind yourself and your teams about your WHAT – make sure you and everyone in the organisation understands it and can explain it simply and concisely.

(Having said that, at the time of writing my mother still doesn't know what I do, and my children think I work at Google – my five-year-old thought I owned Google for a while! When

I say you and your teams must be able to explain your WHAT simply, I mean to your target market. You can work on your family and friends later.)

What do you do?

What would your immediate response be? When people ask us what we do for a living, we tend to focus on the technical name of our profession, which, if you think about it, means very little most of the time. "I run an agency", "I am a graphic designer", "I'm a developer", "recruiter", "builder", and so on. Instead, we should be more specific. "You know when you look for clothes on Google and you see all those ads from various brands? I do that. I make those appear there". "I design websites and logos for small businesses". "I build software to do XY and Z". "I find good people for good companies looking for staff". "I build houses and commercial properties". I think these are much better answers. In business, talking about what you do in this more descriptive, less prescriptive way is far more effective. Especially when you make it remarkable – more on being remarkable soon.

Check out these examples:

"We exist to deliver a measurable impact on the organic digital performance of the world's most exciting brands. You need to feel safe, yet hugely excited about your agency partnerships. Our intelligent hiring strategy, built on a unique approach to account management, delivers a 95% client retention rate. Something we are very proud of." – BuiltVisible

"We're a team of leading [CRO] experts, specialists in our own optimisation fields, that work together to accelerate your conversion optimisation program through our unique framework." – User

Conversion

"We revolutionise digital marketing campaigns and bring exponential growth to retail brands investing between £30K and £500K/month in digital marketing channels" – Genie Goals

Your proposition statement does not have to contain all of your WHATs. Your value proposition statement should be enough for someone in your target market to understand what you do and ask for more details. If they are reading it or listening to it, they should feel interested enough to find out more. By this I don't mean just curious; they should feel what you do applies to them. In general people are curious – we might find a topic interesting yet not be interested in investing time or money in exploring it because it doesn't apply to us. I might look at a Lamborghini with curiosity but not care about doing the research I might do for a car I could actually afford or want to buy. You want your proposition statement to be a filtering machine that attracts the right audience and makes them want to know more.

What's different?

This is where you focus on how you are different – your unique selling points (USPs).

We deliver relentless growth to retailers through award-winning digital marketing. We've built the technology that helps you grow through smart bidding; Google awarded it the most innovative in EMEA. We have built a team of super-specialists with 13 native languages who can help you create winning strategies and take your brand to the next level, anywhere in the world.

Let's break this down:

- Multi-award winning = credibility.

- Specialising in retail = major USP, as at the time of writing, Genie is the only retail-specialist digital marketing agency (to the best of my knowledge, and if not the only one, then one of very few).

- Most innovative according to Google = major USP and credibility, as only three percent of agencies are at our level according to Google.

- In-house technology = mid-level USP

- 13 in-house native languages = major USP, as at the time of writing I have not come across organisations with more than three.

Now compare it with something like this:

A London-based digital marketing agency.

Welcome to [Agency XY], a digital marketing agency based in [location], London and [location].

Our honest and transparent digital marketing work speaks for itself. We deliver a personal, passionate & tailored service to each and every one of our clients, big or small, based in London or abroad.

We strongly believe that there's no merit in a 'one-size-fits-all' approach to SEO, Content Marketing, Social Media or SEM. Our digital marketing methods are innovative and always anticipate the intent of your customers and search engines.

If you want clear, honest and tangible results online with the opportunity to learn how they're achieved then get in touch now to see how we can help.

This isn't super bad, but it certainly isn't as compelling as it can – and should – be. Let's break it down:

A London-based digital marketing agency.

It's unnecessary to say "London-based" as it adds absolutely zero value and can be stated elsewhere on the website, making the information easily accessible if the customer wants to find it. There are gazillions of agencies in London, so saying that you are based in London is like telling a person you want to date that you wear shoes when you go out.

Welcome to [Agency XY], a digital marketing agency based in [location], London and [location].

Welcome to [Agency XY] is waste of attention that could have been directed elsewhere. The logo, the URL and the branding around the website say the name already. "... a digital marketing agency based in [location], London and [location]" is an unnecessary repetition of an unnecessary piece of information.

Our honest and transparent digital marketing work speaks for itself.

The moment you mention you're honest, you put the idea in people's minds that one might be dishonest. People, at least in the UK, believe you are honest by default – your case studies, accreditations, references, and current clients will show that for you. "Our honest and transparent digital marketing work speaks for itself" is a weak statement. It doesn't speak for itself, we know nothing about the work. So unless it's connected to a case study the customer has supposedly just read or seen, that sentence means nothing.

We deliver a personal, passionate & tailored service to each and every one of our clients, big or small, based in London or abroad.

Personal service? Passionate? Tailored? These are things the customer expects. These are things that any other agency can and will say. Can you imagine an agency's team responding to the questions from a customer who asks: "do you provide a tailored service? Are you passionate about what you do?" Who would ever say: "not really, we don't provide a tailored service and we don't really care about what we do"? The value proposition must tell people the stuff that isn't obviously expected, the stuff that they need to hear to understand how you are different – in our case, retail only.

We strongly believe that there's no merit in a 'one-size-fits-all' approach to SEO, Content Marketing, Social Media or SEM. Our digital marketing methods are innovative and always anticipate the intent of your customers and search engines.

The first sentence is about something they don't do, and which they don't believe is good (one-size-fits-all). It's better to describe what you do and how you do it. For example: "We conduct a strategy session with each of our amazing clients, during which we design, build and plan the most effective approach and campaign engineered to deliver on the exact KPIs that are important to you."

We've learnt this the hard way and, whilst surely still not perfect, we have made some progress. Here's how we would approach it:

We revolutionise digital marketing campaigns and bring exponential growth to retail brands investing between £30K and

£500K a month in digital marketing channels.

When you work with us, you choose a multi-award-winning digital marketing agency specialising in retail. You choose one that, according to Google, is in the best performing three percent of agencies in the EMEA. And you choose a partner that produces results no one else can through our combination of unique in-house technology, bold strategy and a retail-obsessed team with 13 native languages.

Most of this is made up of tangible differentiating points that tell customers exactly how we are different to most others. It also acts as a filter, as it tells non-retail brands and brands with less than £30K a month to invest that we might not be their best choice.

The point here is to illustrate exactly how you are different from the alternatives. Do not attempt to describe yourself as better than or superior to your competitors, as this can and probably will produce the opposite effect – no one feels good or inspired when an organisation says they are better than another. And by talking about 'the other', you are drawing attention there instead of to your own solution. Importantly, by describing the negative elements of your competitors, you are eliciting a negative feeling. That means the person you're engaging will experience your brand alongside that negative feeling you elicited, even if the negative comments were about another organisation.

Focus on yourself and on the things that genuinely make your solution different. Rather than saying "better", or "more efficient", simply state the things that make you better or more efficient and let the customer draw the conclusion. This part of your proposition must focus on articulating clearly and succinctly why you are remarkable. We will talk about creating a remarkable proposition soon. Once you have built a remarkable proposition, you must illustrate it clearly in your proposition statement.

What's remarkable?

If you are running or thinking about starting an operation that you want to grow to a remarkable level, you have the responsibility to create something remarkable.

Let me plead with you [*praying hands*]: please don't start just another [fill in the blank] just for the sake of 'taking a slice of the cake'. The cake always ends up tasting fucking disgusting. There are few things as sad as starting a venture just to copy something that already exists. It's the saddest thing in the world.

I'm not suggesting that you should only create totally revolutionary businesses or products, like the new touch-screen, smartphone or self-driving car. But if you already run or want to start a digital marketing agency – or a construction company, a plumbing business or any other service business (though this is true for most products too) – then you must at the very least believe that you offer something remarkable, different and unique.

If you simply copy what's already being done, you will probably live a very miserable life, competing on price, spending tonnes on marketing just to make more noise than everybody else, and watching as all the passion is sucked out of your mission.

Instead, strive to create something remarkable, something unique. And always strive to create a remarkable experience for your customers and staff. Here are a few examples:

Google:

- It's freaking Google. It changed everything for the better. The world is easier with Google.

- As part of their green initiative, Google rents goats to mow the lawns of their mountain view HQ.

- Google employees in the US get death benefits. This guarantees that the surviving spouse will receive 50 percent of the employee's salary every year for a decade.

- In 2004, I made a mistake with AdWords and spent £1K in one day. I asked for a refund and they gave it to me, even though it was my mistake.

- Mission: "To organize the world's information and make it universally accessible and useful."

Tesla:

- Electric cars that are sexy.

- Renewable energy focus in everything they do.

- Mission: "To accelerate the world's transition to sustainable transport."

Amazon:

- One-hour delivery (mind-boggling).

- One-click shopping.

- Super-frictionless shopping experience.

- Buy anything from A to Z.

- Mission: "Our vision is to be earth's most customer-centric company; to build a place where people can come to find and discover anything they might want to buy online."

Zappos:

- 500 in-house customer services employees based in Las Vegas: focus on customers – for real.

- Once they ran out of a product and instead of telling a customer they had run out and leaving them with the problem, a rep travelled to a competitor's store, bought the shoes and delivered them to the customer personally.

- They sent a bunch of flowers to a customer who, whilst on the phone with Zappos to find out how to return an item, said she suffered from a condition that made her feet hyper-sensitive and therefore could not wear the shoes. They sent a note in the flowers wishing the woman well.

- Mission: "To provide the best customer service possible. Deliver WOW through service."

Apple:

- Revolutionised the mobile phone by creating a radically different smartphone – all others followed. Even though the touchscreen technology already existed, by improving it and applying it to mobile phones, Apple revolutionised not only the tech and the mobile phone device, but also the way we consume information and communicate.

- Mission: "Apple designs Macs, the best personal computers in the world, along with OS X, iLife, iWork and professional software. Apple leads the digital music revolution with its iPods and iTunes online store. Apple has reinvented the mobile phone with its revolutionary iPhone and App Store and is defining the future of mobile media and computing devices with iPad." Interestingly, they often use a much better statement at the end of press releases: "Apple is committed to bringing the best personal computing experience to students, educators, creative professionals and consumers around the world through its innovative hardware, software and Internet offerings."

Ryanair:

- The first real low-fare airline – allows people to travel for less than a meal for two might cost.

- More flights in a day than some airlines do in a week.

- Loads of destinations.

- Mission: "To offer low fares that generate increased passenger traffic while maintaining a continuous focus on cost containment and efficiency operation."

And it's not just the big boys:

REV.COM:

- I used REV.COM to write parts of this book, and many others have done the same. Speak into your phone (I have a strong Italian accent), click one button and 24 hours later (often much sooner than that) get an accurate transcription for very little money.

HUEL:

- Complete food replacement – each portion provides 100 percent of your recommended daily allowances (RDAs).

- Made a meal replacement product cool, ethical and trendy.

- Amazing and personable customer service.

Genie Goals (of course I was going to put this in):

- Performance-only model: alongside a traditional charging model, Genie Goals offers a pure performance model. If the client doesn't make money, neither does Genie Goals.

- Builds bespoke technology for clients.

- Works with retail brands only.

Rolling Dojo – Brazilian Jiu-Jitsu academy:

- Parents who can't afford normal rates pay what they can afford.

- World champion instructors.

Cape-to-Cuba – Restaurant in South Africa:

- Everything in the restaurant is for sale: the chair you sit on, the table you eat at, the plates… everything.

What problem are you solving? The Stripe case

I had the pleasure of interviewing Nick Beighton, CEO at ASOS[1], who shared with me the advice he always gives to young individuals who want to be entrepreneurs:

"You must solve the customer's problem. It starts with solving

---

1 Interview with Nick Beighton, CEO at ASOS https://lucasenatore.co.uk/16-minutes-with-nick-beighton-ceo-at-asos/

the customer's need."

That's the core of this section. Many startups fail because there's no demand for their product, no problem to solve. Stripe did have a problem to solve – a big one.

The world's financial infrastructure is very old and clunky. For years, the e-commerce industry suffered from poor solutions that allow businesses to take payments from users securely and smoothly. The traditional solutions took forever to get implemented and the fees seemed endless. The problem was that nobody dared develop an innovative tech solution for an industry as heavily regulated and institutionalised as banking. The result was the banks were deciding what the market needed. PayPal was around but its main focus and purpose was to facilitate the transfer of funds from friend to friend, before becoming the number one solution for the eBay marketplace. But there was still a massive gap in the market; the industry needed hackers, and banks aren't hackers.

Enter Patrick and John Collison. Born in Ireland, the two brothers felt the pain and began the process of turning the world of online payments on its head. Their final solution was simple enough to be built by two brothers and yet powerful enough to change everything. The final result was a short code (seven or twelve lines – debatable – but either way still freaking short), which would enable e-commerce businesses to plug the solution into their webshops, instantly connect it with their bank and take payments from credit cards. Easy implementation, fast integration, low fees, and the ability to take payments online without having to wait weeks and spend hundreds – all of this was a product of the two brothers' work and innovative thinking. The embodiment of less is more. They called it Stripe.

Unsurprisingly, Stripe was a massive hit almost instantly, and many global startups began using it. Stripe became a vital part of many organizations' financial operations – including Facebook. As well as solving an important problem, the two brothers gave themselves a strong WHY and a mission that was bigger than just profit. Their mission is to increase the GDP of the internet, and to achieve that, they are thinking beyond payments and writing software that helps organisations handle payments to their staff, detect fraud and, I suspect, many other functions.

Stripe wants to change the way online payments have worked for more than twenty years; the company wants to give people with good products or services a chance to compete with bigger organisations. Co-founder Patrick Collison said to Bloomberg[1]: "We think giving two people in a garage the same infrastructure as a 100,000-person corporation – the aggregate effects of that will be really good."

The Collison brothers dropped out of college in 2009 to start working on what would become Stripe. They set up an office in Palo Alto, California, mixing in with the various startup giants like PayPal. When Stripe was launched in 2011, it took the industry by storm, mainly because of the ingenious simplicity of the solution to a gigantic problem. With Stripe, all an organisation had to do was add seven (or twelve) lines of code to their website, and voila! They could now take payments online.

Before Stripe, this would have been a very expensive project that took several weeks. Now, no more than cut-and-paste. Before Stripe, finance teams were in charge of choosing the payment gateway. Now it was in the hands of developers, thanks to the Collision brothers.

Stripe changed the way the financial industry operates in

---

1   https://www.bloomberg.com/news/features/2017-08-01/how-two-brothers-turned-seven-lines-of-code-into-a-9-2-billion-startup

regard to online payments, which was something no one else would have aspired to do at the time. This is why the Collision brothers struggled to raise the capital to grow at the beginning. Tech startups loved Stripe, but potential investors were sceptical, mainly because it was hard to believe that a group of techies could change such a traditional and heavily regulated industry. They all thought that if any organisation could make that change, it would be PayPal. Ironically, PayPal co-founders Peter Thiel and Elon Musk loved Stripe and invested in it.

Stripe helps more than 100,000 businesses deal with online transactions, processing tens of billions of dollars in transactions annually. Stripe went from 80 employees to 750 in three years. They charge a fee on each transaction, which makes Stripe a very interesting business, valued at a massive $9.2 billion at the time of writing.

Examples like these of companies that created something remarkable are abundant, but the list of companies that didn't is almost endless. Whether you build something in an existing product or service space that goes radically beyond what anyone else is doing, put a new spin on an existing service, create a new variation of one that's revolutionary and valuable (like UBER), or create something that doesn't yet exist (like Stripe), you must aim to build something remarkable. The alternative is just too boring, and, simply, very likely to fail.

Be different, solve real problems and be remarkable!

Actions

- Take time out to answer the following questions (make sure you come up with strong, compelling answers):

1. What's your value proposition? What do you do?

48

2. What's different about it?
3. What's remarkable?
4. What problem are you solving?

THE PLAN

One of the most misunderstood and misused tools I have come across in two decades of building businesses is goal setting. It is mind-boggling that the vast majority of people with any sort of ambition, in business or otherwise, fail to set and execute goals in a structured way. According to the 4th Annual Staples National Small Business Survey, more than 80 percent of the 300 small business owners surveyed, don't keep track of business goals. This turns my brain inside out. How the fuck is anybody going to achieve anything if they don't even take the time to decide what they want to achieve?

At risk of stating the obvious, I feel I have to mention how unbelievably important it is to set goals. Not setting goals is like embarking on a long drive to an unknown destination, without sat-nav or directions of any sort. Setting goals badly is like having half an address and using an outdated system or map. If you don't set goals, you are hitting a golf ball without knowing where the hole is. If you set goals badly, you're hitting it with a broom. Into football? Not setting goals means there are no goalposts and you're kicking the ball blindfolded; if you set them badly, you're playing with wellies on.

Okay, no more analogies: if you are building something remarkable (and if you're not, why the hell are you still reading this?), not setting goals means you're working towards something unknown; this will inevitably force you to take a short-sighted approach, which will cost you time, money and opportunities. Setting goals badly will reduce your chances of success many-fold.

Set goals, and make sure they're important; think about what you want to do now, but also about your ultimate goal. How is your big WHY encapsulated in your goals? Twitter used to say that they wanted to reach every person on the planet. To achieve such a lofty ambition, every goal must somehow contribute to this.

So for goodness' sake, take the time to set goals – or better, set OKRs.

GOALS

There are many goal setting methodologies, and one of the most commonly used is SMART goals. This framework has been around for a long time and it certainly offers massive benefits and useful guidance.

The SMART framework was introduced by Peter Drucker, a management consultant and author, whose work contributed to the foundations of business management as we know it today.

The SMART methodology offers clear guidance in writing goals. It is led by the criteria behind the acronym, which stands for:

- Specific

- Measurable

- Achievable

- Relevant

- Time-bound

Let's break these down:

Specific

"Grow the agency" is not specific. "Win X new clients, each generating a gross profit of X per month/year, and win X awards" is much better. Being specific simply means being as clear as you can – if a stranger who has no idea about your goals only reads the S- part, they should know exactly what you want to achieve.

Measurable

When and how will you know that you have achieved the goal? This is where you include indicators of progress and success, and specific milestones.

"Win X new clients, each generating X gross profit by X." This is the Smart and Measurable version of our original goal.

Achievable

If it's humanly possible then it's achievable. You should focus on creating a goal which is hard and ambitious but humanly possible. By 'humanly possible', I mean that if any other human, in your circumstances, with your resources, could do it, then so could you. That's about it. It's hard to put more conditions on it than that. Ambition is not only fine, but required – as long as it is humanly possible, then you are on to something achievable, as far as I'm concerned.

Yahoo told Larry and Sergey that it wasn't possible for yet another search engine to succeed, but look at Google. If I had shared my goals with people who knew me 20 years ago, nobody would have said I could have achieved them. This happens all the time – people set out to do things most others, including us at times, don't believe are achievable, and they achieve them anyway. You might be one of them, perhaps after finishing this book.

Relevant

Your goal needs to be aligned with the bigger picture, your mission and other goals you might have. It's also important to ensure it is aligned with your values. If you're running a digital agency and its mission is to engage millennial customers on the latest social platforms for clients in the fashion industry, a goal to launch a computer literacy service for seniors might not fit. If you are a marketing agency running a project to help reduce people's debt, as part of your social responsibility campaign, then aiming to win customers in the financial industry might be against your values.

Time-bound

When will you achieve the goal? There is always a 'tomorrow', a 'next year' a 'next quarter'. Being specific with your goals' deadlines allows you to move at the right pace with the right urgency and be able to measure your progress. Knowing when to change strategy, adjust, and sometimes even quit is vital.

This last point is not strictly related to SMART goals, but it applies to most projects: knowing when to quit. If you are building something new, innovative and really revolutionary that has not been done before – and this can be a way of doing things, a new piece of tech or simply a new marketing strategy – it's important to persist and be resilient but also to know when to quit.

How do you decide when to quit without running the risk of quitting too early? Imagine this: you invest all your money in digging machinery because you know you've found a spot in the desert above a river of oil. You dig for months but no oil can be found. You quit, sell your machinery to a scrapyard man and go home defeated. The scrapyard man pays a professional expert in the local mining industry who tells him that at that particular spot the oil vein makes an atypical turn and it's forty inches to the right. The scrapyard man digs forty inches to the right and gets the oil.

That's what quitting too early can do. But not quitting when you should, could hurt even more if you don't know about the atypical vein route. In this example, the oil miners did lose the oil to the scrapyard man, but they sold the machinery before it was too old and before they were too tired and worn. They went home and started a new business there. Had they waited too long they might have not made any money from the equipment and might have been too worn out to start a new venture.

So what's the correct answer? Like most things, plan the exit. Give the project, the new piece of tech, the new structure or whatever you're innovating and changing a deadline and then call it a day when that comes. Of course, apply your common sense to this but be wary that sometimes common sense gets blurred, especially if we are emotionally connected. The way you protect yourself from yourself is to involve a team – perhaps the board, the senior management team, your mentors or colleagues, depending on your company structure, network and nature of the project. If you are starting out and don't have these people around you, you might involve a friend or family member. Everyone, no matter what their status, needs advice and mentorship. So make sure you have people who can be the voice of reason that helps you make good decisions.

OKRs

Creating something remarkable and different to what's already out there is vital if we are to progress and build a remarkable business. This is true for all things, including management and planning. For goal setting specifically, one of the remarkable evolutions from the traditional techniques and frameworks, such as SMART, is OKRs (Objectives and Key Results).

The OKR framework was introduced by Intel CEO Andy Grove and brought to Google by venture capitalist John Doerr. Today OKRs are used by many companies, including Google, LinkedIn, Twitter, UBER and, of course, Genie Goals (I'll share the guidelines we give managers at Genie Goals for setting their OKRs soon). This very book was written using the OKR methodology.

The basic question we are trying to answer with OKRs is: Where do we want to get to? The point of OKRs is to make sure that we always have a focus on the long-term growth of the company (for MDs and C-suite), of your team (for managers) and for your own project/career (personal OKRs).

OKRs help you describe in an inspirational yet crystal clear way what's important to you as an organisation, team or individual. They offer the right structure to illustrate the road ahead in a way that pushes us to take more risks, because they provide a degree of control and confidence that other goal settings frameworks don't.

From a company perspective, OKRs offer control and transparency. They allow you to see that everyone is working towards a common goal. From an individual viewpoint, OKRs help you form a clear picture of what you need to and can achieve personally whilst contributing to the company goal and also ensuring you are progressing in line with your own ambitions and desires.

The value of setting goals is greatly loaded toward the very fact that we stop and consciously think about where we want to go, rationally. Most shortfalls and challenges are solved by thinking, but we can't solve problems with the same thinking we created them with.

OKRs require you to engage in structured thinking. Much like SMART goals, OKRs force you to stand back and think hard about where you want to get to as an organisation or individual and crucially, how and whether you can get there.

Once the company-level OKRs are created, everything else must feed into these. This doesn't mean that team and individual OKRs must match the company's OKRs, it just means that they have to contribute towards them.

For example, if the company's OKRs are "Achieve exceptional business growth through scalability, use of technology and people development whilst delivering account excellence to provide a remarkable experience for all clients", then as an individual it would be perfectly fine to include in your OKRs something like "Become the best manager I can, through formation and leadership training". You could also include something around learning new skills, networking, speaking at conferences, personal development and more, as these would all feed into the company's OKRs.

Once you have built your OKRs, you will have a super-clear idea of what's important to you, not only that year but that quarter, that month and even more granularly. This has a positive impact on productivity, on the ability to get and stay in flow, on your ability to prioritise and on the energy level it creates in the environment, as everyone will find it much easier to keep their eyes on the prize, even when dealing with unpleasant or boring tasks.

This is the first goal setting framework I have ever come across that offers a useful and effective built-in reporting system. As you will see, the OKR structure offers a fantastic way of planning, executing, reporting and therefore adjusting as you go. It allows you to look back and essentially get data for future decisions.

We've adapted the OKRs to work better for us and I'll detail our methodology shortly. If you are interested in hearing Google Ventures partner Rick Klau talk about OKRs at Google, go to a cafe, grab a coffee and a notepad, and watch the following video (it's 81 minutes long): goo.gl/krqmAK.

Some key features

All OKRs must be public within the company – everyone should have access to everyone's OKRs.

All personal OKRs will be negotiated with line managers and will not be dictated by each individual. This is to ensure that people create OKRs that are inspirational and important to them whilst also contributing to the company's OKRs.

Company OKRs will be discussed at the level of the senior management team or board.

Further features are embedded within each section of the OKRs.

Objectives

Objectives are the ultimate goal, the North Star for that period. We should be able to review the objectives at the end of the period and, without need for interpretation, understand whether we have been successful and to what degree. This should be as close to black and white as possible in terms of the score – a traffic light system can work well for this:

- Green: nailed it

- Amber: delayed/in progress

- Red: missed

(We use numeric scores at Genie Goals, which are detailed soon.)

Objectives must be massive and transformational. They should be risky and make you uncomfortable. They often involve committing time and money to something that may not work and might not happen. If you look at your OKRs and feel super confident you'll achieve them, then you're not thinking big enough.

Objectives should not contain numbers and they should be inspirational.

Time allocations

Obviously, there are different levels of focus on OKRs vs operational tasks, depending on roles and positions within the organisation. More junior staff will typically be spending 80 percent of their time on operational tasks, whereas a more senior team leader or manager may be focusing 80 percent on OKRs.

Key results

Key results are the KPIs of the objectives. They are the things that tell you that you have achieved the objectives. They must be measurable – if it doesn't have a number, then it is not a key result ("made it better" is not a key result).

The only exception is for key results that are binary for things that are either hit or miss, like "launch website".

Annual and quarterly OKRs

At Genie Goals we set annual OKRs which run in line with the calendar year. So you should be asking yourself, for example, "where do we want to be next January?" Annual OKRs are critical because they draw a clear picture for the 12 months ahead but also allow you to set quarterly OKRs from which you will build your roadmap of tasks you must complete.

You can revise your annual OKRs each quarter; they should not be seen as too rigid. However, that doesn't mean you should use them as a backup if you lose confidence, it just means that if something unforeseen happens which dramatically changes the situation, then you can and should adapt. For example, imagine you planned to "become the most influential agency in the UK through winning awards and accounts with great brands" (this would be your objective) and your key results were to win X accounts, X awards and be invited by Google to speak to other agencies about agency growth (BRAG ALERT – I have been invited three times at the time of writing). You're on track, but halfway through your journey you win a massive account in the US which causes you to change focus, for a great reason. In this case, it's totally okay for you to revise your annual OKRs.

Annual objectives may typically be broader or more strategic, as you're looking at the final product or outcome for the year, at the end of which you will set brand new OKRs, which might be (though they don't have to be) totally different and focused on completely different areas of the business.

Quarterly objectives are typically more tactical and more geared towards achieving the yearly goal – they contribute towards the bigger goal and are therefore slightly more rigid and execution-focused. Things like "Test CRM project to establish a new revenue stream" or "Achieve best customer feedback rating and inspire clients to refer us to other clients" could be examples of quarterly objectives.

Grading

At the end of each quarter and year, you must grade your

OKRs. The results should be published within the organisation. Grading is supposed to be quick, you should not need to spend ages doing it. If you have set clear OKRs, grading will be just matter of looking at the statement and putting a mark next to it. No need for much interpretation.

The intention of grading is direction, correction and monitoring, not to judge one's work. Whilst the successful achievement of OKRs may be used during appraisals to compliment your staff, OKR scores and outcomes should not be used as criticism (constructive or otherwise) in appraisals. The point here is to measure and observe what went well and what didn't, to inform future decisions and next steps. If something has succeeded, what happens next? If something has failed, do we ditch it? Try again? Remember the keyword here: **direction**.

The mechanics of grading:

Each objective and key result should get a score between 0 and 1. Here are some example scores:

Zero = complete fail, or OKR just wasn't done
0.6 = satisfactory result
0.7 = good result
1 = nailed/100% result

Key results get a score each and then the objective relating to those key results gets the average score of the KRs. But don't be too strict in applying this. It's easy to imagine a scenario in which you've met the key results, but you still don't feel you've achieved the objective and perhaps, though less likely, the opposite too.

Here it's also useful to include comments as to why you've

arrived at the scores, including lessons you've learned and thoughts on direction.

There are at least two types of OKRs that require a slightly different thought process for grading:

- Some KRs are binary – yes or no – and should therefore get a binary grade, i.e. 0 or 1 (e.g. "launch new website").

- Quantitative KRs should get quantitative results. If the key result was to drive £100k in revenue and you managed £50k, then your grade is 0.5.

When assessing the first two kinds of OKR, you should indicate whether a particular success or failure was due to circumstances that are unlikely going to appear again or are out of your control. For example, a client got an injection of cash and invested all of it with you, which caused you to achieve your targets and without which you would not have done, or a client was sold to a larger group with an in-house team, which caused you to miss your target. You get the point.

Like I said before, don't take OKRs as a way of being measured on your work or measure your team on theirs. They should help you monitor and manage the direction and effectiveness of everybody's efforts. So be honest, be super critical and be proud.

Action

Planning is vital but planning alone is useless; you must take action. Once you have set your OKRs, you must follow through with action. This is why at Genie Goals we have adapted the OKR framework to include a roadmap section, as an integral but visual and structural part of the process. In this section, we list all the projects and steps that are required to achieve each KR. It has a powerful positive impact on our focus on OKRs.

This is what it looks like:

Objective		
KR 1	KR 2	KR 3
Roadmap item 1	Roadmap item 1	Roadmap item 1
Roadmap item 2	Roadmap item 2	Roadmap item 2
Roadmap item 3	Roadmap item 3	Roadmap item 3
Roadmap item 4	Roadmap item 4	Roadmap item 4

A real-life example of this is our Growth/Business Development team's OKRs:

GROWTH Objective 2018: Build and execute a client acquisition strategy which allows us to meet our financial goals, deliver an unbelievable customer experience and help our team develop and grow		
KR1: 17 new services sold in 2018	KR2: GP per client increased to £7.5k	KR3: Increase number of services to 2.0 per client
Send 20 ABM boxes per quarter to Heads of eComm, Marketing Directors, etc. at target retail companies	Write to all clients, communicating new services to them to ensure they are aware of new opportunities with Genie Goals	Create a cross-channel methodology, with the intention of both practically creating coordination at 'Head of' level, and communicating value of having more than one channel with Genie Goals
Meet at least 3 new Heads of E-Commerce or similar target position in target companies per month	During sales process, ensure our proposals are cross-channel where appropriate	Identify opportunities, and ensure that cross-channel methodology is communicated in all pitches and marketing

Deliver on the promise of delivering audit requests within two weeks, but aim to do so within a working week		Build a pitching doc that sells cross-channel methodology
Reach out to 60 target people per week in target roles for target companies on LinkedIn		
Release one video, and one blog post per week on topics appropriate to our target market		
Establish paid social media advertising on Facebook and have it bringing in 5 audits per quarter		
Attend at least 3 industry relevant events per quarter to meet 5 new contacts per event		

As you can see, the addition of a roadmap brings action to the planning framework and allows people to use the OKR documents as guidance in their decision making and direction each month.

Here are a few tips for making the most out of your OKRs:

- Learn your team objectives by heart – everyone in the team should – this is your mission for the year or quarter.

- Look at your OKRs daily – print them and stick them on

64

your desk if necessary.

- Get familiar with other people's OKRs so you can help them and they can help you.

- Talk about them incessantly to your teams, to your colleagues, to your friends and family, and to strangers in the pub (Ciaron's idea).

- Work hard to make your OKRs inspirational; resist the temptation to think small and in the box.

OKR crimes

As you have seen in the Google video (not watched it yet? Do it!), failing to hit OKRs is not a crime. But there are OKR crimes, things you must not do. Here they are:

- Not put in enough effort to achieve them. Failing to get the results you wanted is very different to failing to put the work in. Put the work in and don't let that be the reason you're not achieving your goals. Hard work beats talent any day.

- Not make time and let 'more important' stuff come up. You have a whole quarter to work on your OKRs. If you leave it till the last minute and something more important comes up, then you've screwed up long before the deadline. OKRs are vital, so prioritise them accordingly.

- Not know your objectives by heart.

- Not enforce OKRs within your team.

This was a long chapter on planning; I know it can be boring, but planning is the equivalent of programming your sat nav correctly before you set off, chopping the ingredients before you stick the roast in the oven, setting up the chessboard and pieces before you start playing. I freaking hated planning with a passion – I didn't like coming up with OKRs, organising the sessions, or writing up the notes and all that follows. I am a dirt guy… I like to be in the field, working the soil. But OKRs are vital to my success, so I learnt to love them by focusing on the big WHY.

Whether you decide to adopt SMART, OKRs or any other framework, choose one and invest in planning and setting goals. If you fail to do the planning, you cannot do the fun part, you will most probably not get to your destination, your roast will be weird, and you'll look stupid playing a chess game on an empty board.

As Benjamin Franklin famously put it, "By failing to prepare, you are preparing to fail".

Actions

- Book one day for OKR planning out of the office.

- Download *The OKRs Strategy Session Format* document here (https://lucasenatore.co.uk/okrs).

- Invite all key staff members. Depending on how many people work with you, you might invite all staff, perhaps for certain sections.

- Follow up with all staff members.

- Communicate clearly what the OKRs for the period ahead are.

- Assign owners to roadmap items/projects.

THE PEOPLE

With the right people, you'll go through hell and come out stronger. The wrong people will drive you to jump off the walls of heaven.

If you are reading this book and implementing the few topics we've looked at so far in your small business with around 15-20 staff, then you are probably three years ahead of where we were at your size as a result. At that stage, we'd only just started to look into OKRs and planning. 2016 was the first year in which we implemented and enforced OKRs, and we had only perfected the OKRs by involving the team in their creation by early 2018. Thanks to the strong sense of direction that OKRs provide, we were able to make better hiring decisions, all geared towards achieving the objectives.

Your OKRs will always include something about people. The single most important element that will allow you to succeed and achieve your objectives is having the right people in your organisation. If you do, then you are off to an unbelievable start on your journey, full of excitement, growth, long-lasting friendships, fun and most likely loads of happy clients, loads of cash and success. If you have the wrong people in your team, then your organisation has cancer.

Who are the right people?

"How do you get the right people? Who are the right people anyway?" Good questions!

Let's start with the second: who are the right people?

To understand who the best people to hire are and what traits they have, you or your team need to answer the following questions: What are your 'must-haves'? Outside of specific roles you might be recruiting for, what traits must people exhibit to fit in with your organisation?

At Genie Goals, we talk about being a Genie or exhibiting the Genie Behaviours: a short list of attributes that help indicate whether a person might fit in well in our company. These are:

Smart: Do they get things? When you ask them questions, do they understand the questions and do they provide to-the-point, relevant answers? You'll find that most people who don't know how to answer a question will talk extensively, elaborating excessively on the wrong answer and digging a bigger and bigger hole for themselves. If smart people know the answer to something you ask, they normally give you a concise answer – they get to the point. Really smart people give you the answer in as few words as possible. Smart people who don't know the answer to a question simply say "I don't know" and perhaps explain why they don't know.

Get things done: We like people who do what they say they're going to do. Talk is cheap and you'll find loads of talkers. It's the doers you're after. What have they done that demonstrates that they get shit done? Provided the other boxes are ticked, you're much better off with someone who tried and failed repeatedly than you are with someone who comes with a bag of excuses as to why projects never took off.

Our 'people who are smart and get things done' philosophy was greatly inspired by Joel Spolsky, a software engineer who developed the project management tool Trello and author of the blog *Joel on Software* as well as the book *Smart and Gets*

Things Done (which is where we got the inspiration from).

Eager to learn: This applies irrespective of seniority! You need people who are going to learn, adapt and grow with the organisation. If they don't, they are likely to stay behind and become a misfit eventually. Can they demonstrate that they like to learn? Have they got examples of self-learning and a motivation to learn? Some of the people we hired who went on to progress quickly within the company demonstrated an amazing drive for self-learning. They watched YouTube videos and took online courses on Udemy to learn how to code, run PPC campaigns, blog, build websites, and even print and sell t-shirts. These people are self-starters and self-learners. These are the people you want in your team because they'll do the same for you, they'll learn new things and implement them in their job, you guessed it, making your company better.

Positive: It is so important that you surround yourself with positive people. Trust me, if you have people around you who just focus on and talk about the problems and the stuff that isn't perfect, you are injecting poison into your organisation and your life! You need people who see problems as opportunities to develop solutions and improve; you need people who see the problem and quickly move to talk about how to find or develop the solutions. This doesn't mean that people should ignore issues or stuff that needs to change. If something is wrong, you tackle it. If there's an issue, you drag the fucker to the ground, you tackle it, discuss it and present it to all who might help you solve it. Then you solve it and then you move on.

The people whose first train of thought is always on issues and stuff that isn't perfect must raise red flags to you, especially when they talk about past issues with excessive negativity and struggle to move on to the next topic. For example, people who criticise their previous employers are to be approached with caution, no matter how bad their circumstances were. It's okay to say that they left because their boss was a lunatic, or because the culture wasn't aligned with their personality, or the development was limited or whatever. The red flag is raised when people go into detail, explain at length how bad it was, and criticise people. Even if it's all true, even if they had a really shitty life, bringing dark energy into an interview with a potential new employer or partner shows a lack of good judgment.

Not assholes: One of the traits that has been pivotal to the growth of the company has been the readiness of all staff to learn from all staff and treat everyone as equals rather than according to their job titles. No one is too senior to fill the dishwasher or make the coffee. Don't get me wrong, having a strong ego isn't a bad thing (if it was, many of us would be in trouble, me first). It's important, though, to treat others the same and never think one is too important or senior to be humble and approachable.

This list of attributes works for us, and I suspect for many businesses. In essence, you want people who are entrepreneurial and have a strong ethos and values which are aligned with those of your organisation. You want to find them and train them further: invest in their learning, send them on courses. At Genie Goals we have developed an internal university we call the Genie Academy. The Genie Academy is a series of 40+ modules to promote cross-learning. Experienced people in the team teach a variety of subjects, from Finance to UX, Sales, Presentation Skills, Editorial Skills, Productivity, Coding and even Mind Coaching. We invest heavily in learning by sending people to conferences and training.

We also give all staff 20 percent of their time for research and development. This is important for several reasons:

- It allows our teams to learn what they are truly passionate about. This helps them stay motivated and excited.

- It brings new skills and opportunities to our business. On several occasions we have seen members of staff come back with compelling arguments to start new channels which we then went on to sell successfully, adding value to our customers, our staff and our bottom line.

- It's a wonderful opportunity to produce content for our blog, which helps establish our agency as competent and as an authority in our space. People doing R&D and then producing reports for internal use can use the same material for the blog, newsletter and other external communication.

- It's a good way to help staff distance themselves from the usual work which often results in renewed energy when they get back to it.

I have encountered countless business owners who squeeze every single billable hour out of their staff and ask all the wrong questions. The worst one is: "What if I spend all this money training people and they leave?" To that, I ask: "What happens if you don't and they stay?"

A Ferrari is a beautiful car, but it turns out it doesn't do too well off-road. Neither the Ferrari nor the terrain are inherently bad, they're just not compatible. The best candidate in the wrong organisation is like a Ferrari off-road. It pays off in the long run to hire only those who tick all your company's personality trait requirements. If you get this wrong, you're in trouble, but if you get it right, you're on to a hell of journey – even when the going gets tough, you'll have fantastic people around you to carry you through the storm and come out the other side, screaming victory: "We have made it!"

Where do you find the right people?

When we officially started Genie Goals in 2013, I was the only non-British person there and 95 percent of people came from within 15 miles of the office. Today we have 13 international languages and probably 20 foreign staff. We didn't find these people, they found us. We focused on building the most amazing place to work we could. We entered employers' awards and took part in job fairs. We gave talks to students at universities and we made working at Genie Goals so good that all our staff went home at night and raved about their jobs and the company. We made people come to us.

When we started looking for foreign staff, we hired many graduates from Anglia Ruskin, an innovative global university with students from 185 countries. Anglia Ruskin contributes to making Cambridge one of the most cosmopolitan cities in the UK; this, coupled with the fact that we invested in making Genie a great place to work and told everybody about it, made it easy for us to find and hire great people from all over Europe.

We used to write a job advert, put it on our website, share it on our social media channels and in a couple of local online directories, and boom! We'd fill every recruitment event, never with fewer than 10 great candidates filtered from a list of 20 or 30. In a single week. Often, during the 'wash-up' session, in which we would discuss the candidates after the interviews, the problem wasn't selecting the right people but rather selecting who to let go as they were all so good most of the time. We used to interview people – and bear with me on this – in a pub. Yes, you read that right. We arranged, and still do, all junior executive interviews speed-dating style in a trendy pub. All the shortlisted candidates would be invited to the venue where they would spend ten minutes at each station, designed to address different areas. They would move on to the next station at the buzzer, and a new candidate would move in. We'd leave a few minutes between candidates but not long.

The stations were:

- Interview about the company, the story and the mission.

- Interview about the role specifically.

- Excel task. Here we weren't looking for defined Excel skills, but for problem-solving skills and whether they understood how to move on the platform. For example, they might be given certain metrics and asked how to work out earning per visit (EPV).

- Written task. Here's an example: *"Genie Ventures are a finalist for Employer of the Year award. In 15 minutes, in English, please write a short entry piece on why Genie should win. Things you might like to consider: Products under Genie Ventures; Clients we work with; Culture of workplace (do feel free to be inventive, this doesn't have to be factual); Our services; Benefits for staff (again do feel free to use your own ideas)."*

It would take 40 minutes for a candidate to complete the process. Each station would score the candidate on a scale of 1 to 5. In the early days, we'd score people on just a couple of elements: mainly knowledge of the company, company fit and

73

the two practical tasks, written and Excel. Then we were blessed massively with the addition of Sarah Sutton to the team.

Sarah is a fantastic individual and a talented professional who took on the role of Head of People and tasked herself with making Genie the absolute best place to work for anyone interested in what we do. Sarah's projects were, and still are, both many and large. From creating a compelling career framework that inspires our staff to promoting a culture of coaching and continuous development, helping managers coach their teams, promoting diversity and everything in between. One of the things that Sarah helped us refine was the way we scored people, making it more accurate and more useful in helping us find the right people. The end result was a clear list of attributes that we could score people on using the same 1 to 5 scale. These are:

- Communication: Did they maintain eye contact? Did they express their ideas? Did they listen actively?

- Motivation: Did they display energy and enthusiasm? How much effort have they put into the interview process? Are they engaged with the world around them?

- Problem Solving: Did they analyse the problem? Did they identify cause and effect? Did they try and find a solution?

- Planning: Did they arrive on time? Have they achieved personal goals and objectives?

- Teamwork: Did they interact well with the group? Do they partake in any group activities such as charities or sports?

- Adaptability: Do they adapt well to change and a diverse group of people?

- Company Fit: This is in terms of cultural / team fit and relates to how you feel they will present themselves within the team/business, do you feel they'll integrate well?

We would have candidates arrive 20 minutes apart, then after they had all gone through every station we would do our wash-up session and decide who we'd hire on the day. We would call the selected people immediately to give them the good news; their reactions gave the hiring team the best feeling.

This works very well for us. As we grew, we changed the process slightly – I stopped going to the speed-dating sessions and the winning candidates would be offered the job pending meeting me and Ciaron for the final stage. We had figured out a hiring machine, at least at the junior exec level, and it worked very well for us. We could fill vacancies on demand.

Then the Brexit vote happened and things changed. We had to adapt to the fact that fewer and fewer people would move the UK as their future would be uncertain. Like most things, the biggest problem wasn't the changes in regulations, but rather the fact that nobody knew what the regulations were actually changing to. This caused uncertainty in the minds of young professionals, and the influx of applications decreased dramatically.

We started conducting first interviews over Google Hangout/ Skype and created a two-stage process: if they impressed us during the long-distance interview, we'd invite them to the office, paying for flights and accommodation, and conduct the rest there. At the office, the candidate would meet different people in the company and do similar tasks and sessions to what they would have done during a speed-dating scenario. We would only see up to three candidates per day and take longer to hire them. When a candidate was successful, we would often pay for the first couple of weeks in a bed and breakfast, if they hadn't yet found longer-term accommodation.

Things had to change because of Brexit – we had to adapt and we had to evolve. Like most things in business, and in life really, having to change makes you better, as it forces you to look for creative new solutions, which often end up being much better than what you were doing originally. Change made us better. It made us work even harder on building the absolute best place to work, as we felt we had more responsibilities towards our staff who would move country (that's freaking amazingly flattering to me) to join Genie. We wanted to make sure we did our part to make it not only worth their while but to help them find the closest thing we could to a new family. I'd like to think we did that. During our last anonymous staff survey, 100 percent of our staff would recommend working at Genie. We have now opened an office in Germany and we're looking to open more in Europe next year.

We are the sum of the people we surround ourselves with, so choose your teams carefully. Don't fill roles, hire great people. Roles change – a role you're trying to fill today is likely to be a totally different role in a few years. You might find the perfect fit for that role today, but without the personal attributes you need, once that role changes and the team member fails to adapt or grows bored, you might be in trouble. If you hire smart, adaptable people who are aligned with your values and non-negotiables, then you can put them anywhere in your company and they'll do great.

How do you motivate your team?

As you build a team of great people, you must assist them, help them learn, give them the opportunity to grow and become autonomous.

Many studies have been conducted on the topic of motivation, one in particular by Dan Ariely, one of the greatest economists of our time. Ariely and three of his colleagues tasked undergrads at Massachusetts Institute of Technology (MIT) with one exercise that required some minor cognitive skill, such as adding up numbers, and another task that required only mechanical skills, namely tapping a key as fast as possible. The students were offered a large or small financial reward for best performance.

The results were surprising: If the task involved only mechanical skills, the rewards worked as expected: higher rewards resulted in better performance. But as soon as the task called for even basic level of cognitive skills, performance was negatively impacted by the high rewards.

Financial rewards, it turns out, only work for very straightforward tasks that are simple to do and require little or no creative or lateral thinking. Whenever creative thinking or cognitive abilities are required, financial rewards and incentives just narrow our concentration and kill our out-of-the-box thinking. You can call it pressure, call it whatever you like, but the end result is that performance worsens.

It's safe to conclude that a financial incentive isn't always the best motivator, it isn't always the best tool to get the job done or to get the most out of people. Especially in an agency environment, where creativity is one of the top skills and attributes that people require. A careful distinction though: people need to be paid fairly in the first place. Whether you use industry benchmarks or another way to determine what's 'fair', you need to ensure that the money discussion is met face first. People need to be paid fairly and have opportunities to earn more. This includes perks, bonuses, etc. If the company does well, then everyone does well. That's a given. What I'm saying here is that additional pay doesn't seem to work as motivator with complex tasks.

So how can you motivate people? How can you motivate your teams and yourself?

In his TEDGlobal 2009 talk "The puzzle of motivation", Dan Pink[1] confirms Ariely's view that financial incentives are not only ineffective at improving performance, but produce the opposite result and hurt performance. In his book Drive: The Surprising Truth About What Motivates Us, Pink argues that the key factors that truly motivate people are:

* Purpose

* Autonomy

* Mastery

Purpose

We find that what motivates people at our organisation, as well as in our clients' teams, is a shared higher purpose. A larger view, a shared vision of what they're trying to achieve. If people understand, are aware, feel part of, and are excited by the mission, then they are more likely to go the extra mile to deliver their best performance. They're more likely to stay up at night and scratch their heads when things aren't going well, and celebrate your victories with as much passion and excitement as if they were their own – which indeed they should be.

This is very much connected to having a big WHY that goes beyond materialistic goals. These do not talk to your teams, they only talk to your bank account. Important missions and

---

1 American author of several remarkable books, including Drive: The Surprising Truth About What Motivates Us, A Whole New Mind, To Sell is Human and Free Agent Nation.

goals, like "Creating the absolute best environment for people to work in, grow personally and professionally and be as happy as they can be outside their homes" speaks to people's hearts. "It's our goal to be Earth's most customer-centric company where customers can find and discover anything they might want to buy" (Amazon) or "Google's mission is to organize the world's information and make it universally accessible and useful" speak to people's hearts, or at least seem to have people's interests at heart.

When you grow, it becomes increasingly harder to communicate the vision and to make sure that the goals, objectives, and direction are shared with everybody in the company. So, my biggest suggestion to you is to build and establish effective communication habits that allow you to communicate effectively across the organisation. If you come up with a mission you intend to last the lifetime of the company, or simply be your objective for the year, then commit to it. Print it out and stick it on walls, include it in all documentation and written communication vehicles as appropriate, and start and finish all staff meetings, speeches and announcements with that sentence. That is how you keep it alive and fresh in people's minds.

One way in which I do this at Genie is to do weekly video updates. At the time of writing, I spend 60, 70, sometimes 80 percent of my time outside of the office. I discovered during a 360 review that one of the things the people, our staff members, wanted from me was more clarity as to what I was up to and what projects we had in the pipeline – stuff that wasn't yet confirmed, but that we were working on. That was a clear request from them to understand more; they wanted not only a shared vision but also to be aware of the stage we were at weekly. I thought this was brilliant, a great piece of feedback.

So I started to record 10 or 20-minute videos most weeks to do exactly that. I share with people what my week was like, where I went, why, and what I was going to do. I would touch on the projects that were not official but that we were working on, and I would also cover slightly higher-level subjects to do with our mission statement, our challenges, our desires for the agency and anything else that could help them develop passion and excitement for the vision. And the results were remarkable. People felt very sympathetic when I was out on business and struggling with something, people reached out to offer their help. It had an incredible impact, both in terms of the spirit of the organisation and in practical terms. People generally knew what we were talking about at any given time, they were on the ball, and it was much easier to get help and to get everybody to buy into what we were doing.

Autonomy

Another thing that motivates people is autonomy, having decision-making power over what they're going to do. So, if you're into any kind of micromanagement, I would strongly recommend that you walk away from it, because it doesn't work. Give people autonomy, let them turn up and decide what they're going to work on.

I recently had the pleasure of meeting a remarkable person called Daniel Hulme, who runs Satalia and also runs an MBA program in London. At Satalia, Daniel was able to establish a culture where people turn up for work and work on what they really want to. They have no fixed projects, and they can literally work on whatever project they want to work on. When I asked Daniel how he makes sure that even the most boring projects get attention, his answer was remarkable. He said: "Well, everybody knows that if we don't work on the smaller or on the less exciting projects, then eventually we'll struggle financially. And if we struggle financially, there won't be a job, there won't be a company, so they do it."

At Satalia, Daniel built a completely flat structure where the traditional pyramid-shaped structure has been flattened to the ground. They have no managers; people manage themselves. People also make their salary recommendations public. Each person tells the entire organisation what they believe they should be paid and everyone else then votes as to whether they should ask for more, less or stay where they are. This is probably for another book, but the point here is that Daniel took the concept of autonomy to the extreme, and it worked.

What's remarkable about Daniel and Satalia is not only the company's non-hierarchical structure, which is amazing in itself, but Daniel's courage to actually set up the organisation that way, where there's basically no need to manage or control people and their workloads, and where people can go to work and choose what to do. He built a decentralized company, a group of people working towards the same high-level goal, which is to enable people all over the world to do things that they really want to do whilst improving businesses through AI and ML solutions. I find that very remarkable.

What Daniel did is unique, and I'm not suggesting for a moment that you should do that. I think Daniel and his team are making it work, among other reasons, because that's their mission: to create a world where people are free to do whatever they want to. So they dedicate all their efforts to achieving that, starting in their own team. Our mission isn't the same, and I feel that creating such a unique structure requires full commitment. But that doesn't mean we should stick to traditional structures and approaches either. The point here is to walk away from micromanagement and give people as much freedom as you can to do their jobs within the structure and scope of your organisation.

We have adopted a solution somewhere in the middle, and we learn from people like Daniel and his team, so we can slowly move towards a more autonomous environment. We give people the overall objective and let them run. Try it yourself. If you do it for the first time, apply some caution and some oversight, and provide people with support, but really resist micromanagement and walk away from the obsolete 'if you want something done well do it yourself' bullshit. Walk away from management altogether and work on coaching instead. Ask people how they're feeling, where they're struggling and help them find the right solutions. Help them train their creative problem-solving minds and resist the temptation to 'fix it' for them.

Mastery

Once people have a big sense of purpose, a shared collective mission that helps them keep their eyes on the prize, and the autonomy to get on with the task at hand, then you're doing absolutely amazingly. To continue their journey, then, people need mastery: the ability to get the job done. This is also known as the concept of flow, first introduced by Mihály Csíkszentmihályi, a Hungarian-American psychologist, in 1975. In simple terms, flow is being 'in the zone' – the mental state you reach when you are so immersed in a task that time goes by super-fast, your focus is super-sharp, and you are simply flowing through the task, with no resistance, no boredom, no force required, it's just happening. In flow, you are so absorbed that time and space fade away.

In order to be in flow, you have to be engaged in a task that has a level of difficulty that's optimal for your level of skill. If the task is too easy, you get bored and can't get into flow. If the task is too hard, you feel it's out of your league and you can't do it, so you can't get into flow.

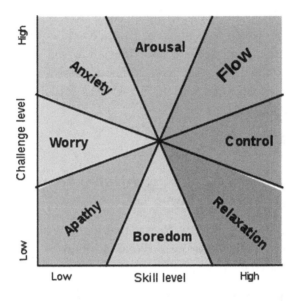

Image source: Wikipedia

In order to help people get into flow, you can give them the autonomy, but they need the skills. This is one of the many good reasons why we must invest in people development, professional and personal, continuously. At Genie, we have a team dedicated to learning and development. At the time of writing, they are at the end of a large project building an e-learning platform for our staff. It's costing us thousands. We incentivise people to go on courses; these cost money and time. We allow people to spend 20 percent of their time on R&D. These are probably the best investments we are making.

It comes back to that question: "Yes Luca, but what if I spend all that time and money training people and then they leave?" And the answer is always: "What if you don't and they stay?"

Make sure you allow people to work towards mastering their skills so that they feel equipped to work on higher-level problems, gain the confidence to choose how to go about solving them and get into flow. That's how you work toward mastery, which, coupled with autonomy and a big sense of purpose – your organisation's big WHYs – leads to massive motivation that lasts.

Actions

- Write down the attributes and behaviours you want your staff members to share.

- Design an interview format that allows you to measure how candidates score on your attribute and behaviour requirements.

- Start thinking about, and jot down on paper, what you can do to promote purpose, autonomy, and mastery. These are likely to be provided by:

  - Purpose: Your why from the WHY chapter; your OKRs.

  - Autonomy: Finding the right people and interviewing them to make sure they are truly the right people; trusting them with small things first and increasing that trust as they get more comfortable; ensuring they are free to fail and make mistakes without feeling scared; letting go of the control you might feel you need.

  - Mastery: Investing in their training.

THE WHERE

When it comes to the WHERE, there are two main points: WHERE to set up and WHERE to sell. There's not a massive amount to say about where to set up or run your operations, but what is there is important. Approaching this strategically can make a massive difference in many ways.

Where to set up

We are based in beautiful Cambridge and that's where we'll stay, at least the HQ. But from the very beginning, from the birth of the company, we were convinced that we would have to open an office in London. All the big agencies were in London. When talking about agencies, our potential customers would talk about London agencies as a separate breed, a group of higher-level agencies – much like you and I might refer to German cars as inherently better. Even to this day, when people find out that we have more than 60 employees at Genie, they are surprised to hear we're in Cambridge; there just aren't many agencies or internet companies of this size around here. We are the largest digital marketing agency in Cambridge and the second biggest digital agency in town. It's atypical to find agencies with more than 20 people and there are only one or two with more than 40.

Opening in London has been on the plans for a long time, but I remember not being convinced that it would be the right move for us. Being in London would have made us just another London agency. Yes it would have given us that initial tick in the 'being in London' box, but as soon as you tick that box, you are in competition with everyone else. If you see a Lamborghini at a Lamborghini meetup, or in Bologna, where they make them, it's still pretty but the effect is not the same as when you see one driving by in your neighbourhood, where it stands out more.

I have a beautiful pair of Michael Jackson Gucinari shoes. Nobody pays much attention to them when I'm in London, Amsterdam or Berlin, I might get a few comments but that's about it. I live in a small village just outside Cambridge. Once I had to go directly from work to a school fête where my wife and kids were waiting for me. I was wearing my MJs. I got there and people reacted as if I had walked onto the school grounds naked with a python twisted around my body, covering my private parts. You could see some parents and teachers elbowing the people next to them and pointing at my shoes. I stood out like a sore thumb – or a naked Italian with a snake on his shoulders.

At Genie, we're not looking for such a shock factor, but we certainly stand out, partly because we're based in an atypical location for agencies. We began being known as the Cambridge agency. We looked for anything that could help us build a good story around being in Cambridge. It's known as one of the most important university cities in the world, and as a hub where super-smart people are bred. A few people who studied at Cambridge:

- Paradise Lost author John Milton

- Evolutionary theory pioneer Charles Darwin

- Broadcaster and natural historian Sir David Attenborough

- Theoretical physicist Stephen Hawking

- *The Huffington Post* co-founder and editor-in-chief Arianna Huffington

- Actress Emma Thompson

- Founder of the multi-million-pound business Cobra Beer, Lord Bilimoria

- Legendary actor Sacha Baron Cohen (Ali G, Borat, Bruno, etc.)

- United Nations High Commissioner for Human Rights, Prince Zeid bin Ra'ad

- Businessperson, poet, journalist and much more, Stephen Fry

- And of course, the smartest guy I know, CTO at Genie, Paul Goodwin

One of Genie Goals' USPs was our technology. We, and by 'we' I mean Genie's CTO, Cambridge PhD Paul Goodwin, developed a complex piece of technology that was initially designed to bid on Google AdWords at a very granular level to maximise both volume and ROI from paid traffic, but was developed to do many other mind-boggling things which we'll talk about a bit later in the book.

So being located in one of the smartest cities in the world and having developed Clarence, one of the smartest tech applications (we went on to win an EMEA Google Award for it), began to form part of a very strong and interesting narrative. We became THE Cambridge agency. People actually started talking about us as "the Cambridge agency with the smart people who developed Clarence".

Fast-forward a few years, being in Cambridge is not only an asset because it makes us stand out from the crowd, but it's also an asset because we can easily hire fresh graduates. As one of the largest organisations in the digital space, students hear about Genie way before they need a job, and once they do, Genie is often at the top of their wish list. **Finding good people who want to work with you is much harder than finding good customers**. Being in Cambridge and being one of the most sought-after organisations in town makes it a hell of a lot easier to attract talent.

Choosing Cambridge as our base, our HQ, has been one of the smartest moves we could have made.

There are pros and cons of being in Cambridge, just like there would be anywhere else. Including London. In London there are many more senior candidates as there are many more agencies. But that also means your employees are being targeted by your competitors daily. It doesn't matter how good you are to your employees, it doesn't matter how many perks and benefits you offer, your competition will offer more money and might paint a beautiful picture of what it's like to work for them, and you will inevitably lose people you spent years training. Of course, if you create a remarkable environment for your staff and follow some of the tips I shared above, you're more likely to retain staff. The point is that it'll always be harder to retain staff where staff are likely to be targeted by many with compelling offers, at least on paper and in the short-term.

I am not saying that if you are in London, Milan, Paris, Berlin, Amsterdam, or any other major city, you should get out. What I am saying is:

1. You don't necessarily need to be in a major city if you don't want to be, you can succeed even out of a small town.

2. Don't be afraid of being different, embrace it and set a new trend.

On the other side of the coin, if you set up in a remote area that's not very well connected, you will struggle. It takes me less time to get to central London from Cambridge than it takes some of our London-based clients to cross the city from the outskirts and meet me there. One of our clients based in Northern Italy, a €120M-a-year company, is based in a small village 20 minutes outside Venice. Venice is beautiful, but after a one or two-day visit you're done – the novelty wears off and you're left in the small surroundings which, trust me, don't offer much. The company is very successful but one of its challenges has always been finding and keeping talented people. It is a global company so finding international people is super hard because nobody in their sane mind would choose to relocate to their HQ; there's very little there for young, multilingual, talented professionals. They have been talking about moving or opening up in the UK for exactly that reason – to solve a problem which, if not solved, could severely compromise the company's growth, especially as technology and internationalization become more important elements of growth.

So make your choice carefully when it comes to setting up your base; don't fall into the trap of following the masses, but be practical. If you are in Bath, Manchester, or Peterborough, for example, make that part of your story if you can, and you really can most of the time. Is there anything quirky about the location? Anything you can make part of your brand? If there is, use it. If there isn't, then simply ignore the location. As long as it is practical – in particular, easy to get to and good for hiring people – you can focus on other more important areas.

Actions

- Spend some time thinking of the unique features and perks of being based where you are. Can you use any of it to your advantage? You might think about marketing or branding, relationships with local universities and schools, or unique things you can take your customers to.

- Also ask yourself, if you are small, will there be space to grow? Will you find the right people there?

- If your customers are not based where you are – for example, you are in London but all your customers are up north – could moving save you much in rent? If you did move, would you still be able to find talent?

THE SPEED

The best time to start something is always in the past. The second-best time is now.

Once you've planned, done your OKRs and ironed out your proposition and how you're different, or once you've decided on the changes and evolution you're going to embark on, you just have to get going. Start, get moving and launch stuff. The roadmap that came out of the OKRs must inspire action – an idea without action is like a table with no legs. If you're building a website, go out with something, don't wait till it's perfect, you must learn to fix the plane as you fly it.

Moving fast pays off, most of the time. This is true not only at the beginning but especially as you grow. When you get bigger you will also inevitably get slower, and speed, or lack of it in this case, really does kill. I am obsessed with speed, and I truly believe that it's one of the most important attributes that has enabled me, and the organisations I have been involved in or built, to survive hard times, beat the competition, and succeed.

When I was running my first marketing consultancy agency in the UK, I'd landed a contract with a giant FMCG organisation and I didn't even have a website yet – I'd never delivered the training they wanted me to deliver to 97 of their employees. We signed them up and worried about that later. At Genie, we signed a contract with a global luxury retail brand when our website was really not in its best shape. It was originally designed when we were much smaller and hadn't yet figured out exactly what we were going to be. Our proposition (which we looked at in the WHAT chapter) was all over the place, or rather nowhere. We didn't have strong USPs, values or a mission, and it all showed on the website.

I remember getting back to the office after signing them up and, convinced they hadn't seen the website, because I thought such an important brand would never sign up with an agency with that kind of image, I rushed to get our designer to publish an improved version of the site as quickly as she could, in case they visited it and changed their minds. The site we ended up with, v2, wasn't perfect, far from it. It was built in just over a week, in-house, by one person. But it was better than what we had, and we felt that if the customer had looked at it then, they might have had constructive feedback for sure, but it didn't make us look like a total misfit. I later found out that they had looked at it, and they did have feedback, and whilst they really welcomed our rebrand a couple of years later, they had not been put off by our earlier v2 appearance.

We knew that the most ideal outcome for us was to have a website and a brand that would make our luxury brand customers proud of working with us, so they wouldn't be reluctant to share the site and refer us to others. But at the time we didn't have the time or the resources to do this. **The choice is often not between better and perfect, but between better and nothing.** This seems widely accepted but rarely practised. Speed is vital, perfection isn't.

I talk to an enormous number of brands every week, and I can see projects as they spiral. Numbers become bigger and more and more people get involved. The teams become bigger and the vertical line that goes from the person doing the operations and the person authorising the decisions becomes longer and longer. Information that travels along that line inevitably takes longer to move from one end to the other. Simple tasks and projects become much larger than they need to be. Ever tried to organise a surprise party for a mate? Just finding a date in the calendar that works for five people can take weeks and tempt you to ditch the friend whose birthday it is if that means you don't have to deal with it anymore. More than five people involved, you're fucked.

If you are a brand and want to test a different a product category landing page, you'll talk to a couple of people in a 30-minute meeting and in the 31st minute an action will be agreed to instruct the development team or agency to do something. You'll test on a small portion of traffic. If the test is successful, you'll refine the look and feel, get approval for a global rollout and you'll be done.

This is what should happen, or close to. But a larger brand would have to go through anything between three and ten people to get this signed off. And the same goes for projects that are pivotal to the success of the brand, sometimes as small as implementing new tech, remarketing or tracking tags, adding filters to product pages and other things that could greatly impact performance. Stuff that takes little time and money to do often takes ages to get approved.

For larger projects, the hurdles can be of stupid magnitude. Imagine you work at a brand and spot a great opportunity to take on the German market. You do your research – market size, competition, payment methods, delivery, postage and packing, industry benchmarks, competitor landscape – and you cross all the 'T's. You build a business case and you send it to your boss Laura, the E-Commerce Manager. Laura sends it to her boss, Dick, the E-Com Director. Dick sends it to his boss, Karen, the Global Head of E-Commerce, and she gives it to the CEO in the next board meeting. Six, maybe eight weeks might have elapsed. It will probably take another two to four weeks to come back to you with feedback. If it comes back down with a yay or nay answer you're done in eight to twelve weeks. It never does. Questions and feedback normally follow. You might find that because of the large disconnect between the top and the bottom, some of the questions will have to be answered more than once. This can go on forever until the energy behind the project is so low that all you want to do is sit in a corner and watch Michael McIntyre clips until you cry. In large organisations, it can take anything between two weeks and six months to get a project off the ground – I have seen that shit happen, I swear. It's absolutely mental, ridiculous.

As an agency, you're unlikely to grow to that extent. Some of the brands I'm referring to have 2,000+ employees, but even those with a couple of hundred employees are often in very similar circumstances, facing similar delays. And, whilst companies with 20-40 people are much faster than the giants, they are still much slower than they were when they had 10-15 people. Ironically, larger companies have the ability to get the job done much faster than smaller entities because they have more contacts, more cash and more people, all adding value to the project. The problem with speed when organisations grow is always – and only – in making the decision to do something.

Whether you set your goals following the OKR framework as it's described in the previous chapter, or any other framework or methodology which gets you to the same end result, you are 50 percent of the way to making and keeping your organisation fast. The quarterly OKRs and the roadmap do that for you. The aim here is to ensure that you establish an environment in which being agile, fast, and able to do in days what others to in months becomes the core of your culture, of 'how we do things here'.

As your agency grows, you need to fight to keep agile and, whilst OKRs, planning and roadmaps are great tools for doing this, the main weapon you have, the most powerful tool that will make you faster and keep you that way, is your agency structure and psychology around processes and projects. Most organisations that grow large get slow; this means you have to move differently to most large organisations. In the following sections you'll find some practical steps to help you get and stay fast.

WHYs and missions

Here we're going to revisit some of the points from the WHY chapter as well as the section How do you motivate your team? I'll add some additional tips and there will be some repetitions. This is intentional because the topic is so important – read it, it's worth it.

You start by making sure that every single person in the company knows and understands your WHY and the mission. Your second step is to ensure you communicate these frequently. This way you have total alignment and you get the buy-in from everyone. Here are a few ideas on ensuring your WHYs and mission are understood and remembered:

- Hold monthly or weekly staff updates and include the WHY and the mission at the beginning and at the end of the presentation.

- Include the mission as part of the value proposition, if possible, on the website, in presentations and in all material for external and internal use, including OKRs.

- Put inspirational signs and wallpapers in the office showing your WHYs.

95

- Include your WHY on the careers page of your website and use it in the interview process.

- Record a video explaining your WHY and your story and use it as your flagship video.

If your team understands the WHYs and the mission and these are cemented firmly in their minds, you're much more likely to get buy-in from them when you present new ways of doing things, including being fast.

Put speed in your OKRs

If you feel you need to focus on getting faster, or perhaps you just want to approach this proactively, then make speed a company OKR. Your quarterly OKRs about speed might look something like:

- **Objective:** Build a strong culture around being agile and maintain maximum speed of execution to keep us and our clients ahead of the curve whilst maintaining the highest quality of service – The SPEED Sweet Spot.

  - KR1: Form a team (or person) who owns the SPEED project; project owner(s) spends 20% of their time on R&D to find ways to get and stay fast.

  - KR2: Reduce turnaround time from idea to decision to X days or less.

  - KR3: Reduce turnaround time from decision to start to XX days or less.

If you achieve something similar to this OKR, you have already done more than 90 percent of what other agencies and businesses have done, and you have, in actual fact, already built a solid plan to get and stay fast.

Ownership

Just like that last OKR suggests, if you want to get and stay fast you must assign ownership of projects to people and teams. If you don't, if you want to steer the ship the whole way, you'll make the journey very long and painful, and you'll limit the distance you can travel. You might get miserable too. This is related to the autonomy part of the section How do you motivate your team?

If you have a solid recruitment and training methodology, one that allows you to hire people who share your company's behaviour and ethos and train them so they become skilled and able to truly understand, live and breathe your company's culture and mission, then you should be able to assign ownership to projects with great confidence.

An owner is someone who drives the project. They might still check with their line manager or someone else before 'pressing the button', but in theory, what they decide is what you'll go with. This doesn't mean that you shouldn't offer feedback or thoughts and suggestions, but these must be fact rather than opinion-based, and should be presented in a coaching manner rather than as dictated actions.

For example, if the owner of the SPEED OKR proposes to find an outsourced team of developers in Europe to carry out some of your more time-consuming development work, you shouldn't just say "no" because you don't like the idea. You should instead ask good questions that help the owner answer the most critical questions and which might lead them to reflect and consider things they might not yet have thought about. You should certainly offer feedback based on your experience, knowledge, and even concerns. But then let the project owner go away and come back with answers; your job is to equip them to help them make an informed decision, not to make the decision yourself.

In short, you have to let go of the temptation to control everything and trust the project owner. Remember, you never agree to 'forever' stuff, you can always agree to trials and adjust later.

Onboarding and paperwork

Onboarding new clients is a very exciting process because you've just won a new client. But it's also one that can take an excessive amount of time and slow everything else down. There are a few things that can help you streamline the process of onboarding new clients.

The first is signing the contract. You pitched for the account (we'll look at pitching later in the book). You won it. You're excited and now you have this bureaucratic hurdle that you have to get over. This is something we've got wrong in the past, and there is still more work that can be done here at Genie to streamline the process of getting contracts signed, but we are in a much better place than we were.

Signing the contract can grind things to a halt and sometimes even break the deal. A contract needs to be done professionally, but it also needs to be simple. For several years we managed to get by at Genie with a contract pretty much written by me with the input of a couple of colleagues. A page and a half, very simple – probably too simple – with not much legal protection. Thankfully, we never had to test it. However, when we started onboarding large organisations, ones with legal departments, we ended up signing their contracts instead. Our contract was a bit too simplistic for them. The lesson here is that it's worth investing early in a legal team. If you are a small business, then a third-party firm can help. All you need is to create a template agreement that you can use with confidence.

The most important thing about using external lawyers is to make sure they understand what you sell, how you sell it, and the various risks involved. You need to make sure they understand how your business works so they can spot risks you might have missed. They also need to understand exactly what you need in the contract, so that they don't include unnecessary clauses and sections. By default, when you go to a lawyer, they will give you as much standard advice and templates as possible. That's not always a good thing. Yes, of course if you have all the standard clauses and sections, you'd probably be covered for every single occurrence. But the downside of that is that many of the sections and clauses may not be applicable or relevant to you or to your potential customers, which makes for unnecessary reading and checking, as well as making the document unnecessarily long. Remember, you need to remove any friction between you winning the deal and the customer signing the contract. Unnecessary sections within the agreement can cause unnecessary stops and obstacles. Make sure that you brief the legal team so they know the exact scope of service, what you need to be covered by and what the real dangers are.

The most important things for a digital marketing business are:

Staff poaching

You don't want clients to be able to just hire your staff, because your staff, your people, are the single most important element of your success, which will allow you to create an environment that you like spending time in. You invest time and money in training or recruiting your staff, and you want to make sure that they don't get poached by clients. When they see how good your team is, some customers with whom you might not have been able to form strong relationships might want to keep your staff. Make sure that you have a clause in your contract that protects you against customers offering your team roles in their organisations. This is what we came up with and have used for a number of years:

"Genie Goals' staff are its most valuable asset. If you were to engage or try to engage our staff without our agreement, we would suffer serious loss. The Customer and the Supplier agree that for the Term (or Extended Term where applicable) and for one year after termination of this Agreement, neither party shall solicit the hiring of individuals who were employed or engaged by the other in providing or receiving the Services under this Agreement."

Payment terms

Another very important element of the agreement is payment terms. Make sure that your payment terms are clear and they are somewhat standard. We have a 14-day payment term in our contract, which isn't very standard – standard is more like 30 days. But in the UK, 14 days isn't outrageous at all; some organisations even ask for 7 days.

We are flexible with the 14 days, and it often gets pushed to 28 or 30 days. We know there's a provision. We know something can happen and it's a straightforward thing to change. But we decided to leave 14 days as the default and play it on a case-by-case basis. Depending on where you are in the world, if you are too far from what's standard and you're not flexible, you might end up hitting a roadblock.

Earlier this year, we onboarded a very large €750M-a-year brand. Their HQ is in Italy, and in Italy the standard payment term is more like 90 days, certainly no less than 60. We proposed that we would accept the 60 days but invoice 60 days in advance, thereby essentially solving the problem, and they accepted this easily. In large organisations, the person you're talking to understands you, they are on your side. They are only enforcing a rule created by someone else which is now embedded in their policies. This is why they're often happy to accept alternative ways for you to get to the solution; as long as they don't break the system or go against the policies, you're okay.

With this customer, we knew that 60 days was not going to be an effective payment term. It's a massive Italian company where things move more slowly, and if finance teams do their job well, things move much more slowly when it comes to paying out. That means payments come in about 90-120 days after invoice. We were invoicing in advance, but we'd still be out 30-60 days. For the first year, we had to take it on the chin and just have our cashflow suffer. We were in a position where we could afford it. You need to be very careful making a decision like this – cash is king, and if you run out of cash, you run out of oxygen and will probably die.

To add another layer, we were absorbing the media spend as well, which means that we had invoices outstanding for between £100K and £300K at any given time with this one single client. This isn't a situation you want to get into, whether you can afford it or not. For us, this customer was very important for many reasons, so we wanted to win it. But we had some strong assurances – we knew they would pay, so it was only a matter of cashflow, not trust. But we also knew that at some point we'd have to change the arrangements. Less than a year since signing the contract, we have brought the payment term down to 30 days.

101

Make sure the payment term you decide to offer is aligned with what you are prepared to be exposed by and what's likely not to be a total surprise for your customers. Know your non-negotiables and only budge if you are comfortable with the risk of not getting paid in time for two or three months – it can and most probably will happen at some point. Protect your cash. If you run out of cash you will fail. You might have the best proposition in the world and the most revolutionary, innovative, cutting-edge product or service, but if you have no cash you have no future. No cash, no anything. Kaput. Large organisations know this, and this is why they will always try to get extended payment terms.

Know your non-negotiables, run credit checks and be prepared, look after your cash, keep a good buffer in the bank, buy your new car next year. Think outside the box. What can you do to mitigate the risk? At the very least, get credit insurance if the cash that you're owed on a regular basis can have a detrimental impact on your business. Very roughly speaking, credit insurance can cost anything from £5K to £50K or more, depending on your business risks. If you sell to organisations based abroad, the costs can be double that. It all depends on the type of clients you work with, your payment terms, whether you pay the media spend on behalf of your clients, and many other factors.

In the last five years, we have probably lost £30K due to non-payment, and this was down to rare circumstances outside anybody's control, including one case of fraud and one brand going into administration. So in our case, the argument is strong for not bothering with credit insurance. It would have cost us anything between £150K and £300K in that period and would only have been worth £30K to us, and that's assuming they'd have paid out. Now we deal with much larger clients and it would be enough for one client not to pay us for two months for the insurance to be worthwhile. So we are exploring again.

Remember to follow your instinct. If you feel that a prospective client is trying to get excessively long payment terms and you're not comfortable with it, then put a firm end to the negotiation and instead invest the time looking for a better client. If something feels wrong it usually is, and even if it's not in the end, you really don't want to take the risk. Remember, one third of startups fail because they run out of cash. You don't want to run out of cash, especially not because of work you have done but not been paid or, even worse, budget you've invested on your clients' behalf which you're not getting back.

All of this slows you down. Get your strategy right and stick with it. You will find elements and notions that will allow you to get and stay fast, and as always, take what fits in with your organisation and what works for you, and drop what doesn't. The goal is to avoid becoming slow, but don't try to get it all done now. Make a start, perfect it later.

Notice periods

This is something that clients, especially new clients, will look at very closely. It's important that you're protected because you don't want clients leaving last minute and causing you resourcing and margins issues. At the same time, you don't really want to keep customers locked in for 12 or 18 months, which I believe is now becoming an obsolete solution.

Many agencies want to be like EE, T-Mobile and O2, trying to lock people in for 18 months at a time. Forget it. It's an illusion, it's silly, and trust me, your clients don't want that, so you don't want it either. I have made the mistake of onboarding two or three clients in the past who were not a good fit, but I'd bulshitted myself into thinking that 'one's gotta do what one's gotta do' to bring in revenue. Bullshit! It came back to bite me so freaking hard that I couldn't sit for six months. We got to a point where we wanted out.

They had come in with a relatively small product catalogue but said that in the following three months it would double, so everything was ready for these additional products to be launched. We forecasted with this in mind under their instruction. The products never came in, but the client expected the same performance, which was obviously impossible – they had limited breadth in their offer and therefore a lower conversion rate (CR). Their attitude to our staff was bad: they were rude, calling 100 times a day about things we had (and were supposed to have) no clue about. They'd change URLs and not tell us, they'd go into the account and change PPC campaigns "just to try a few ideas" and break the whole thing.

Listen, no one is perfect, we have made mistakes with some of our clients in the past, and we still do at times. But these guys were lunatics, they were out of their minds. We wanted out. But they had another four months in the agreement; our agreement didn't make provision for exit clauses under any circumstances. We had locked ourselves into a very bad relationship. The amount of time and energy this account sucked out of us was crazy. It made us slow for that period because we were firefighting, and loads of people were involved, which meant they were not doing other things.

Even if you make provisions in your agreement so that you can get out of situations like this, you don't want to propose long-term agreements because this will almost certainly get some objections from your clients, resulting in some back and forth, and you accepting some mid-way solution. Stuff like this kills speed. There are better things your sales team could be doing – I can think of a few, including finding new customers.

Plus, think about this: imagine you lock a client into a 12-month agreement and, for whatever reason, after six months they are not happy and want to leave. But they can't because you have your bulletproof, telecom-inspired 12-month contract in place. Now what? They are unhappy or need to leave for other reasons but you keep them in. What good can that possibly do? It's like a girlfriend or boyfriend who wants to leave but you somehow keep prisoner. It's safe to say they're not going to get you a Valentine's present. If a client wants to leave they should be leaving, for both your sakes.

Now this does depend on what you sell. If you sell large development projects, re-platforming or anything that takes a long time, then you may get away with long agreements. If you sell something that is extremely front-loaded, and you need to have long agreements because you are likely to be out of pocket for the first few months, that's also okay. Although I would invite you to revisit your business model in that case, because, and I know I'm repeating myself here, even if customers are locked in legally for long periods, in an agency business, clients can usually leave anyway – and you would want them to. Once they want to leave, they have already left, in a way; keeping them locked in because of contractual obligations really doesn't do anybody any favours. When a door closes, in business as well as in life, another door opens – a better one. When a customer wants to leave, they want to close the door. Let it close.

A few years ago, we started moving from the standard 12-month agreement, which generated some objections, to a rolling 90-day agreement. That took away 100 percent of the objections and presented us with 0 percent downsides. We had absolutely no repercussions.

Having a shorter-term rolling agreement does a few things: The first is that it removes any objections from the legal team, who are trained and briefed to object any long commitment in the agreement. The second is that it communicates to the wider team in your customer's organisation that you are confident you will provide a good service, because your agreement reflects that – it's saying to people, "Hey, we don't really need to keep you locked in for 12 months because we're confident that you will want to stay." And third, it provides flexibility.

It also helps you meet expectations and fix problems. When things get difficult, and sometimes with customers they absolutely do, if you have a rolling 90-day agreement, you can easily get that one last chance. It's easier to persuade a disappointed customer to give you one more term. Customers will forgive you and give you one extra chance, which will help you make things better if something is going wrong.

Compare that to what happens when the going gets rough on a 12-month agreement. Even if the client signed it easily, as soon as you have a hard quarter where performance is down, even for reasons that are perhaps not under your control, then the customer will be very quick to put their notice in because they don't want to be locked in for another 12 months.

Having a 90-day rolling agreement is a subtlety that has really made a big difference to the speed at which we recruit new customers and get contracts signed, but also in terms of retaining clients and maintaining the image of our agency.

Making a change like this will take away almost all chance of objection to contract length during the onboarding phase, which in turn results in tonnes of time saved by all parties. More time for you to innovate, win new business, and grow. This is SPEED.

Exclusivity

The other point in the agreement that is important for us as a digital marketing agency is exclusivity. We request that during the period that we are working on the account, no other agency works on the same account, doing the same thing. The reason is very simple, and two-fold: firstly, we are innovators, so we do things differently. We push the boundaries. We are in the top 3 percent of Google Premier Partner agencies in the EMEA. We have access to BETAs, and we do things other people don't do. We also develop technology, and quite simply, we don't want other agencies to see what we do as we're doing it. This book is for sharing what we've learnt, but tech is different – we need to keep developments closer to our chest.

Secondly, we simply don't want others tamper with our work. If things go wrong, and when too many hands work on the same cake they do, who takes responsibility?

Other agencies will always approach your customers offering them a free audit of the account to see if the current agency (yours) is doing a good job. Frankly, customers should take these offers up, because it's never a bad idea to get an account audited. If an audit does reveal something that looks wrong, it's never a good idea for the customer to jump ship right away – it's better to confront the agency working on the account and see what they have to say.

It's a healthy process, but we don't want agencies to come in and do an audit without us knowing and see the way we work behind the scenes. If a customer asks, we will provide the agency doing the audit with certain access so that they can audit the account without looking deeply into what we are doing. Certainly we don't want agencies to start tampering with what we are doing, which is why we don't want an agency on the same account offering the same service. We're trying to avoid people touching the account when we're working on it, because it's then very hard to understand whose responsibility it is when things go wrong.

Service levels and travel expenses

Another thing that worked very well for us in the agreement is the service level. Here we list the stuff that we are contractually obliged to do in terms of service beyond strategy and execution. Things like:

- Weekly reports

- Weekly calls

- Monthly meetings

- Quarterly business reviews

- Email and phone assistance

You want to make sure that you indicate who pays the travel fees. If you have a client that is based abroad, who pays for the travel when you go to meetings? How many meetings are you contractually agreeing to? That's very important, because if it's not specified, you may find you're travelling way more often than you intended to, and you might see your margins sliced at the end of the month. Travelling can be very expensive, even in within your own country.

We have clients all over Europe – in the Netherlands, in Italy, in France – and even if we only send two people abroad for one night, booked on a budget airline and in a modest hotel, we're easily looking at £1,500 to £3,000 depending on whether we need to take the client to dinner, and so on. And that's not to mention the out-of-office time. If you pay for the meetings, if these costs are included in your fees, then you need to be very specific as to how many meetings you are paying for. It's better if the client pays travel expenses on an ad hoc basis, although you still need to be mindful of the out-of-office time.

The main message here is to be aware of these things. Don't let them become sticking points, but be aware of them, because this is where you'll create discrepancies between what you thought you were going to make and what you see in the bank. And most brands, especially larger ones, have absolutely zero problems paying more, so do your numbers and then charge more. We'll come back to this later.

GDPR

Most of this book will remain relevant for many years to come, but I don't know if I can say that about the GDPR section. At the time of writing, the EU General Data Protection Regulation (GDPR) is painfully relevant for any agency operating or working with clients in Europe. It's an important thing to consider in the agreement, so make sure you add a GDPR section to your template terms and conditions that tells the customer what data you collect and what you do with it, and make sure they agree to what you expect of them. We had to stop working with a client because their setup was incorrect and meant that we were receiving personal information about their customers, including email addresses and credit card details.

That covers the main points of the agreement template. Make sure that you have noted all the points that are relevant to you, to your business; the ones that I've talked about here are relevant to us. Get this out of the way early and you'll tick a massive box, and it will take the risk of getting roadblocked by bureaucracy.

Roles

Another element in the process of onboarding new customers that will make your life incredibly easy if you do it right and incredibly hard if you don't, is establishing roles. Once you have agreed to work with a new customer (although this may not be applicable if you're only just starting), ideally, you will want to assign owners to the next steps to move the project forward.

Once we get the big fat 'yes', we need our tracking tags implemented on the customer's website – a string of code that allows us to measure performance. There's a team that will drive that forward. There's a team to look at agreements. The team assigned to the account will organise the pre-launch meeting, arrange the weekly calls, and manage all the stuff that needs to happen before anything else can happen, before we roll.

This is easy to arrange: as soon as we agree to work with a new customer, we send an email to all the people involved. We introduce people by name and role, not necessarily their title within our organisation, but their role within the project, and we start the group conversation. We do this by email, but tools like Asana, Trello or any other collaboration tool work well too.

Then in our customer relationship management (CRM) software, we assign the next action to each person. That way the process starts and there are several people doing several bits, all contributing to the collective goal, with a centralized record in the CRM. That way we can keep control over all the parts that need to come together.

Before we established this process, we had one person who spent ages coordinating everything and arranging meetings, tracking tags and collating all the information and requests to then send them to the customer in one email. The thinking behind this was to keep the communication with as few people as possible for the sake of controlling processes. What total control freaks we were! Putting all these bits together and just send everything in bulk to the customer seemed tidy from the customer's perspective, but it actually caused massive delays, as information was bouncing from one person to the other. Writing this down makes me realise how absurd it was.

With our new and improved method, after the verbal agreement is reached, we introduce all the parties involved, and everything moves very, very, very quickly and very, very, very smoothly.

There is obviously much more to onboarding and project management; countless books have been written on the subject, offering all the details. But for the sake of achieving speed when onboarding new customers, this is really all I would have wanted to know a few years ago, and all you need to know to get faster. There might be exceptions depending on what you work on, what type of business you run and what type of customers you have, but in general terms, I think this is the 20 percent of the information that should cover 80 percent of the needs of 80 percent of the agencies out there.

Reporting

How much time do you and your team spend reporting? We talked to a number of agencies that admitted that some staff members spent more than 10 days a month manually pulling all the data to form a report and answer clients' questions. That's 50 percent of someone's time spent working on something that already happened.

Obviously, reporting is important, and if done correctly, it's vital for understanding what dials to move to improve performance. Reporting is also very important for keeping clients in the loop with what's happening and with the results they're getting. And it's a way to talk about the activities that your team completes on the account, including the experiments that didn't work.

Clients love to see a team that's engaged and not afraid to admit failure. One of the things that most retail brands said to me during interviews I carried out while writing this book is that one of the things that most annoys them is when, during meetings, agencies focus excessively on the small wins, which are of arguable value, and try to hide or underplay the mistakes and things that didn't go well. Customers want to see transparency and are far happier when we admit that results are not good if we give them good reasons and a strong narrative and tell them exactly what we are going to do to improve performance.

Reporting is also a great opportunity to upsell new services, but you're not going to upsell if the client doesn't trust you.

There are things you can do to make your life easier with reporting, whilst continuing to add value for your customers.

What's important now?

Ask each client what's important for them to see in the near future and focus on that weekly. Clients may ask for full reports but then only look at the same three or four metrics. During the onboarding phase, and then during each quarterly business review (QBR) or meeting, make sure you ask your clients what they want to see on a weekly basis, and build your reports mainly on those metrics, only reporting on other areas as and when something notable comes up. This does not mean that you don't monitor the other dials – you have to do that so you understand performance. What it means is that you don't spend time reporting on things that aren't important now.

For example, we've just done a strategy session with one of our customers and the conclusion was that for the next three months at least, they want to focus on aggressive growth. They want to engage in brand-lifting activities, drive new users to the website, grow their email database with their website traffic, and increase revenue from new customers as much as possible. We have decided to reduce the return on ad spend (ROAS) targets and go after growth for the next few weeks. We'll then review the strategy later on in the year and adjust. This is a common growth strategy in e-commerce, and it's proven to speed up growth.

In this scenario, we won't include large paragraphs on efficiency, conversion rates, cost per click or cost per thousands. The data is still there; our customers can access these metrics easily. We just won't spend as much time building a narrative around these things because they are not our focus. We will not talk about negative keyword lists extensively. We will not talk about position optimization or checkout analysis. We'll still monitor these, but we won't spend time writing them up. Instead, we'll focus on micro conversions, people signing up to the newsletter, engagement from new users on social channels, time on site, sales from new vs existing customers, email open rates and unsubscribes. We'll look at visits to sites and sources, and we'll look at search reports to see how many people search for the brand, to understand whether the top-of-the-funnel campaigns are working.

We have alerts in place which allow us to monitor everything, but we invest time in writing about the things that matter today. If the focus was efficiency, then we'd probably report on checkout abandonment, competitors' reports on pricing, channel by channel, campaign and even keyword ROI analysis, segmentation, time of day/day of the week, location and gender device bidding report and narrative. As you can imagine, if we were to write even just one meaningful paragraph about each of these things, it would take ages to complete a report. That's why you want to know what's important and focus on that. We have seen many agencies that have given up reporting properly and just send across dry numbers about everything. Unless the client understands the operational part of the channel very well, dry numbers mean absolutely nothing. When reports like that are presented to the Board, they are just numbers and provide zero support for making decisions for the future.

So long story short: monitor everything but only narrate and report on the objective for the near future. Use plain English in your report, and build a narrative that explains succinctly what you have done that contributes to the objective:

- What was the hypothesis?

- What results did you see?

- What will you do next?

- Why do you think these are good next steps?

You can report on more elements during your quarterly or annual meetings, depending on the size and complexity of the account.

At the time of writing, we build custom reports and pull all the data automatically using Data Studio. That means 'all' we need to do is write the narrative. I say all in inverted commas because the narrative takes a good chunk of the time if you want to get it right. As I touched on earlier, irrespective of what the objective is for the quarter or the period ahead, when it comes to reporting, writing a strong narrative should be where you spend most of your time, as it's where you can add the most value, both to your clients and to your agency.

The narrative is where you get to show your passion for the account and the hard work you've put in, which produced both amazing results and flops. You get to talk about the competition, the challenges, and the plan going forward, ensuring total alignment and setting the right expectations. If you include your proposed plan of action for the next period in the narrative, your clients have the opportunity to contribute and won't be surprised or disappointed at the end of that next period. You can also focus on things outside the channels and services you manage. For example, if you manage PPC, you could talk about conversion rate optimisation (CRO) and search engine optimisation (SEO) and upsell those if you offer them.

Make sure you write exciting narratives, even when results aren't good. There's nothing worse than a Word version of the numbers. Say things like:

"We saw an opportunity to increase the revenue by building this campaign because competitor A did X and felt very excited about the potential uplift. We launched on the Monday and performance looked great for two days. Unfortunately, X happened on Wednesday and CR dropped, causing a loss for the week. The team was so disappointed as it looked like a fantastic opportunity. We thought long and hard to find a solution and we're going to do A, B and C. We are confident that this plan will help us make up for the loss and hopefully drive incremental sales in the coming weeks. Sorry this didn't go our way, we find it's important that we try different strategies to stay ahead, and although we know they cannot work all the time, it's vital we keep trying."

This shows depth, passion, and true interest. I have seen

agencies in similar situations either not say anything about the loss-making campaign or blame it on some outside influence. Bad idea. Be transparent, passionate and solution-focused and your clients will love you for it.

If you get reporting right, you will save time for your account managers and also in your entire organisation. Your staff will have the time to do the work that matters.

Automate

Don't stop at automating reports, automate as much as you can. Do you sell PPC? You must automate the bidding at the very least. If I was a client and I knew you were changing bids manually, I'd find it very hard to understand how you were bringing value. An algorithm can do it infinitely faster and, if you choose the right one and set it up properly, infinitely better. As an agency, you bring value in consulting, advising, setting the strategy and coming up with the answers to questions like: "What can we do that nobody else is doing? How do we win?" Changing bids is not complicated, it just needs precision and speed. Tech is better than humans at both of those things. Use tech.

I've seen lots of resistance to and suspicion of automation in agencies. What the hell? Really? Why? You don't need to sign a contract with the Tech Devil and then let it do what it wants to do. Here are the steps to make automation work:

1. Find what your staff are spending most of their time on. A questionnaire, a series of interviews or a close look at a project time tracking tool will tell you.

2. From the list, take the more mundane tasks: the stuff that you could teach a new exec in a day or less.

3. Ask yourself, or better, ask your staff and network of trusted peers: "Are there tools to automate this?" Maybe get a tech lover in your team to 'own' and lead this, and have that person do the investigation and coordination of next steps.

4. If the answer to 3 is yes, go to step 6.

5. If there are no tools, ask your tech team or a third-party software developer organisation: "Can this be automated?" Send them a brief of the problem and they'll tell you pretty quickly whether it's easy, possible or unlikely. Again, your tech-aficionado team member can lead this.

6. Once you have the solution in place, test it – don't just run with it. Test on smaller parts, with loads of supervision and checks, and gradually adjust and learn as you go. Once your confidence level is high, deploy more and faster. You might find you save a ridiculous amount of time, and get the job done a lot better.

Two potential outcomes:

1. If you are (finally) automating something that others in your space have automated for a while, then you have just made your business more able to compete. You've given it a fair chance, because let me tell you, if others in your space had successfully automated anything that you hadn't, you had been hurting your business and your clients.

2. If you are automating something that nobody in your space has automated before, you absolutely fucking rock. And your clients will love you for it. Be honest, be open and tell your clients what you're doing. Some of them might even let you

use them as guinea pigs. We've been there, more than once. Trust me.

Developing tech that might enhance the performance of a core channel for an advertiser or a customer of any sort is true innovation and will set you apart from those who don't: most of your competitors.

I'll use an advertising example because it's my industry, but you can think of an equivalent in most other industries. Remember, it's the principles that matter, not the nitty-gritty.

Millions of advertisers use Google to promote their businesses. Tens of thousands of agencies are tasked with helping advertisers makes sense of and succeed at this and make a profit in the process. The agencies that stand out use what is uniquely theirs (their team, methodologies, and, crucially, their tech) on the advertising platforms. They are essentially developing on the product (Google, Bing, Facebook, etc.) to make it work better for them and their customers. If you do that and you ask yourself what you can get out of these platforms using your tech and talent that others can't, you're on to building a seriously interesting business proposition that doesn't involve thinking up something from nothing, but rather 'turbocharging' existing advertising platforms.

For example, we developed a piece of tech that would automatically create pay-per-click search campaigns on Google using a product feed (a document listing a retailers' products with several attributes – price, colour, size, etc.), which at the time was only used for Google Shopping. The results would show the product image and price as you might see it on Google when you search for a product. This is now old news, but when we built this tech, it was pretty new. It enabled us to take an existing tool (the product feed) and use it on an existing platform (Google Ads – Adwords at the time) and automate the creation of campaigns to cover the customer's entire product catalogue, of 14 million products in this case. To do this manually would have meant several months of very boring work which, due to the low demand for some of these products and the high labour costs, would have probably been unprofitable for our customer. Automating this mean that we could build campaigns for these products in weeks with very minimal manual intervention, enabling the customer to increase revenue and profit with minimal increase in costs.

As you can see, it's not necessarily the tech or the automation that I'm on about. It's more the thinking, the attitude and readiness to think outside the fucking box and make complex stuff simple. Once it's simple you can get a machine to do it.

This is the principle I'm talking about.

Actions

- Make sure your WHY and mission are clearly understood, communicated and accepted by all. Include them everywhere, including presentations and email footers, if you can.

- Look at all open projects and ensure these have 'owners'. Ask: "Who owns (or can own) this project?" Once projects have owners, don't interfere. Help, coach and provide oversight but let them get on with it.

- Build a solid agreement and other documents that might be needed. Invest in a lawyer earlier on if necessary, and make sure your paperwork is solid. It must protect you but should not contain clauses and rules which might cause friction and delay approval if you don't need them in there.

- What can you automate? Look at the section 'Automate' and follow the steps outlined.

SECTION TWO: GROW

This is the largest section of the book, for a good reason. Although building a business is far from easy – it's hard work, it needs your full focus and attention, creativity, passion and commitment – growing a business is even harder.

Growth is about increasing the numbers, improving the processes, selling and expanding, and it therefore requires change. Change can bring resistance and requires a different level of thinking (we'll look at change in section three – REPEAT).

This section is all about how to sell your services, the mindset of selling (which is the cause of most people's failure to sell), the numbers in selling, the 'rejection' nature of the selling game and how to deal with it, and the massive importance of sales.

We'll then move on to how to market your agency, from social media and Google Ads to exhibitions and networking all the way down to how to create the winning pitch. This includes strategies for preparing the pitching deck, how to present, and tips for the actual sales meeting. We'll even talk about the fees you might charge.

Some parts in this section are very specific, some are technical, and some are more about the principle and the idea. Adapt these to your business, adapt them to your current circumstances, target market and to the stage you're at on your journey. Remember, it's never copy and paste.

Enjoy.

THE SELLING

Mindset:

Sell sell sell. When all is said and done, you have to sell. No selling, no cash; no cash, no business; no business, no you... Okay, a bit dramatic, maybe, but you get my point. An incredible number of people start a new business and work extremely hard to build something remarkable and kill themselves to get everything right. Then they ruin it all by not selling – not as in they failed to win business, they don't freaking try. They don't sell. They say bullshit like: "My customers are different", and "My company doesn't do selling the way others do, it's word of mouth". You can be sure you'll see these people change their 'passion' a few times before retiring into employment or building something that just scrapes through and keeps them prisoners of the weekly 7am networking events. All because they failed to sell.

It's not a skill problem, it's not a time problem, it's not a resources problem. It's a mindset problem. The mindset I know most people adopt is that of fear. Fear of rejection. Fear of the 'No'. Wake up and smell the coffee, my friend. There will always be more 'no's than there will be 'yes'es. This is as true for new starters as it often is for larger businesses and agencies. Irrespective of what you're selling, there will always be way more people who don't buy what you sell than those who do. If there are a bunch of people in a room, all of whom could buy from you, the majority won't. This is the nature of the selling game, most prospects will say no, leaving only a small percentage of your prospects who say yes. It's the way outbound sales works. It's a numbers game, and you need to be comfortable hearing 'no'.

It's a numbers game

When I first started in sales as a very young man at 19, I was selling an alternative solution to the Yellow Pages. I'd travel throughout the north of Italy meeting potential new customers – we'd make the appointment via telephone and then I would visit them in person. I'd fill the time in between appointments by visiting other organisations nearby, basically door-to-door, literally walking in and asking to speak with the owner. We knew that for every 100 calls made, we'd set five appointments. For every five appointments we'd sell one contract worth 820,000 Italian lira (old currency; LIRA 820K was the equivalent of £820 today). It was absolutely a numbers game: if you followed the script, if you stuck to the activity, over a reasonable period of time, the numbers would always be the same. Five percent call to appointment, 20 percent appointment to a LIRA 820K sale. It was very tempting to think this wasn't true at times. When you had a bad week you could blame it on the weather, news and whatever else was likely to get you sympathy from others – and from yourself. At times the opposite happened: you'd have a monster week and started to believe you were better than the stats.

I remember once when I agreed to meet a potential customer on a Saturday morning – more like the customer agreed to see me – and I travelled up to Valsassina, a gorgeous part of the region where I used to live, where 80 percent of the companies around were (and still are) cheese producers. I walked in and the owner of the business greeted me and showed me around the whole plant. They were a proud bunch, quite rightly, and showing their business to others was clearly something they did with joy. Being a Saturday, he must have felt more relaxed about time, so the tour was comprehensive. After a brief chat, I walked out with a LIRA 990,000 contract. Above the daily average and 100 percent conversion. Success!

On the way back, I decided to stop at another cheese producer – cold, pure door-to-door, just because it was on the way. What follows wasn't planned, although I admit that knowing they were super competitive with each other, I didn't go out of my way to stop the prospective customer from seeing the name of his competitor when the contract I'd just signed a few minutes before fell out of my folder. I walked out with a LIRA 1,250,000 contract, the next level up from the previous customer. 100 percent conversion rate and three days' worth of sales in half a non-working day. I was flying – that was the Superman role model in me coming out! I repeated this the whole journey down to my home town and ended up with a further:

- LIRA 820,000 from stop 1.

- LIRA 820,000 from stop 2.

- LIRA 1,900,000 from stop 3, this time with a nuts and bolts producer, probably just because I was super pumped with energy coming out of every pore and, you know, success breeds success.

I closed that half a day with LIRA 5,780,000 in sales – seven days' worth of contracts in one non-working half day. That was my record day, record week and record month. But fast-forward six months, the total for the six-month period would have more or less normalised back to the usual five percent call-to-appointment and 20 percent appointment-to-sale rates, because I had sick days and bad days.

The very first thing that one has to do in order to get the right mindset around selling is to realise that selling is a numbers game.

It's not about the 'NO's, it's about the activity

The second thing, equally important, is that selling is also a 'no' game. The majority of the time you will get a rejection, you will get a 'no'. It is vital that you understand and always remember this, because this is the number one factor that will either help you sell more or stop selling. Fear of rejection is the biggest reasons for businesses not selling. They are afraid to get a 'no'; they are afraid to be rejected and perhaps humiliated. This is absolutely crazy, because you will definitely get rejected, you will absolutely get a bunch of 'no's, it's in the numbers. What do you think happened to the 95 percent of the calls I made? What happened to the 80 percent of people who agreed to see me but didn't buy? They said "no". Some more politely than others. There will always be more people saying "no" than there will be saying "yes", and yet many fear the 'no's. Fucking insane, it kills me actually.

As I write this down it hits me even more, how silly is this. It's like setting up a PPC campaign and then panicking when the first 100 clicks don't make a sale! Or sending out 10,000 leaflets and worrying that you only got 200 sales. You have to go through the 'no's to get the 'yes'es.

The number one selling skill that one has to master is the mindset, and part of that is accepting the 'no's. The healthy way to look at this, the only way really, is to take each 'no' as a step towards a 'yes'. Fall in love with 'no's; they are great because they take you one step closer to your next 'yes'. I promise, this is absolutely how it works. It's about the activity. If you stick

126

with your activity, go through the tasks and actions and correct your approach as you get feedback, you will eventually get to your yes.

What you must dread isn't the 'no's, but the 'maybe's. 'Maybe's are your worst enemy; if you let them, they will kill you. We will talk about them in the next part, but first take a moment to focus on developing a mindset that allows you to see a 'no' as a step towards a 'yes'. And remember, a 'no' is just a 'no today'. Many of my 'no today's turn into 'yes'es down the line.

'Maybe's

Imagine you are spinning a plate on one hand. Then you get another spinning plate on your other hand. Now stick one on your head and, why not, one on your left foot too. You're done. There's no more space for another plate anywhere. Now imagine you see a plate with great, yummy food on it. It's yours if you want it. But you can't take it because you're all taken up with the spinning plates.

'Maybe's are like spinning plates: they give you work, loads of it, massive amounts to do, but no return, zero, fucking nada. Every 'maybe' is another item on your to do list: "follow up", "do this", "do that" and so on. Every 'maybe' is also mind space – you think about it, you worry about it, you get excited about. But nothing. They absolutely drain you. And, I can assure you, 'maybe's don't convert. The vast majority of 'maybe's will become 'no's after a long, painful and time-eroding game of cat and mouse. 'Maybe's are spinning plates; drop them all, drop the spinning shit and get on with work that matters.

More on 'No's

When you get a 'no', say thank you, be grateful to your prospect because they did you the massive favour of sparing you from a painful 'maybe'. You should feel about people who give you straight 'no's the same way a samurai feels about the enemy who kills him with a straight, painless hit to the heart. A straight 'no' gives you the opportunity to move on and focus on your next 'yes'. But ask for feedback, always. The way digital agencies typically get the verdict is by email; if you are lucky, you'll get a phone call. Either way, ask for feedback, honest and thorough. How? Just ask! Say things like: "Hey, I appreciate you letting us know, and I'm super grateful that you gave us the opportunity. We fully accept your decision but want to get better. It would mean the world to us if you could spare five minutes to give us some feedback." And then give them the chance to give you specific feedback, brutal feedback. Better verbally, of course, and easier to get at times. If in writing, you can design a Google Form or just send a few questions in an email. You need to work out what these questions might be depending on what you pitched for, to whom, how, and so on. Spend some time designing these questions, come up with stuff that is likely to get answers you can act on, ask open questions: what and how, mainly. A few examples:

- What are the top three reasons you've chosen not to go with us?

- What did you like the most about our pitch?

- What did you like the least?

- How passionate about working with you did we come across on a scale of 1 to 5, and why?

- How did you feel after our pitch?

- What questions or thoughts were you left with after our

pitch?

- If you were us, what would you have done differently?

Don't copy and paste these, come up with your own. You have one shot, one chance to get valuable feedback. Stuff like this can make you a super-agency; feedback can be the reason you pull in your next big deal. But you have one shot, so make it count. And don't you fucking dare argue, don't get defensive, that just sounds pathetic and will close the doors with that person, even when she moves to another company. Don't reply, trying to justify why you did what you did. The temptation will be very hard to resist – I've been there, I've got it wrong in the past and I've done exactly what I just told you not to do (which is how I got the wisdom, so that's my silver lining – I did it for you!). But you must resist. Be respectful of the time your contact put into giving you this feedback, don't waste their time by trying to convince them it was a misunderstanding, trying to convince them you are better than they think, or even worse, asking for a second chance. I have done that too – it's a very, very stupid thing to do.

Years ago, we pitched for what seemed like a massive contract at the time. On decision day, they called us and told us they had given the contract to another agency. "Totally respectful of your decision 'Bob', no problem. I appreciate your feedback. Please may I ask what made you decide to go with Agency X?" "Oh yes of course. We really liked you guys, you came across really well but the other agency had just something extra. For us it was the 'match-type' that did it. You guys were close but Agency X told us they were going to target exact-match as keyword targeting which for us, given our sector, is important because it will help us get the targeting right."

For those who don't know, match-type is a targeting feature

in Google Ads (previously known as AdWords) that allows you to target people when they perform a search using specific keywords in the exact the order in which you specify them in the account. This is very basic best practice; we didn't mention it in our documents because we felt it would have been the equivalent of saying that the new car you are selling to a customer comes with wheels.

What I wanted to shout was: "What the fuck?! Are you fucking kidding me, are you actually insane? You're telling me that you chose them because they... what the actual fuck?!" What I actually mumbled was something about us not mentioning that because it was so basic that we thought it'd be obvious, which clearly went down as an inelegant and grotesque attempt to change their mind. Two lessons I took with me:

1. Don't leave anything out the deck. Our standard deck went from 15 to 94 slides after that event... I am serious. And it works! More on this point later in THE KIS vs THE KIL section ahead.

2. Don't argue. Take the feedback and go home to obsess about it – decide what's applicable and work on it. That's what we did. Our conversion rate from pitching to confirmed skyrocketed as a result.

Be respectful of their time, learn from the feedback you get and move on. Say "thank you" and go get better.

Your 'no's are also very important because if you take them well, they give you the opportunity to establish a great relationship. You must play the long game, though – you must remain patient. If you took the feedback, nothing would be stopping you from sending updates after, say, six months, saying things like: "I thought I'd let you know that as result of your feedback we have changed A, B and C. I just wanted to thank you, your input and help made what we're doing a lot better". You could even say, if it's true: "we recently won X and Y and I can honestly attribute this success to your feedback, at least partly. Thank you". If you were really classy, you could send this as a handwritten letter with a small gift. Follow up a few months later with an invitation to an exclusive event. Keep in touch with genuinely good pieces of content. Do this with a few contacts, and in time, you will see several 'no's convert into 'yes'es.

It took me six months to win a contract with a global wine subscription brand, four-and-a-half years to win a high-end children's furniture and equipment brand and five-and-a-half years to win a great bedding retailer. Play the long game. The approach is different with each potential client, but the point is to stay in touch, keep adding value for those who gave you a 'no', without being intrusive or stalking them, and never lose sight of them. If you are really passionate about their brand, about working with them, this should be easy. Build relationships, even when you get a 'no'. Follow people as well as brands, send them congratulations when they move on. Did they tell you they like golf? Send them a note when the world championships start. Remember, play the long game.

Activity

Martial arts are 20 percent physical and 80 percent mental. Professional fighters who are unbelievably talented often crumble and perform badly because they can't deal with the stress and the nerves. Their minds prevent them from being as good as they are, day in and day out at the gym. Those who are not necessarily the most gifted physically but have a solid mental attitude are the ones who win the most.

Selling is 20 percent about skills and 80 percent about activity. The skills are important, although, today more than ever, buyers are savvy – especially in B2B digital marketing selling – and the old sales and marketing techniques that might have worked previously don't work as well now. Creativity beats talent any day. Truly caring, being able to follow up and build real relationships, and playing the long game are massively important and effective. But the most creative strategy with the most personal touch and warming effect will fail without consistent and continuous activity. Activity beats everything. Activity is king. Bow to activity.

Work out what you need to do first, what activity is likely to produce the best results? Calls? LinkedIn InMails? Handwritten letters? Events? Content on social media? At the beginning you might have to try several approaches and see what works.

Further on, I share some information on techniques and strategies for marketing your agency – I describe the exact strategies I have adopted to grow several businesses, including those we've used to grow Genie Goals from zero to working with some of coolest global brands, being rated by Google as one of the top 3 percent in the EMEA, and being invited by Google to speak in the UK, Germany and Italy to other top 3 percent agencies (which, of course, allows me to self-proclaim us as being at least in the top 2 percent :)). Once you've read that part, come back here and read this again if you need to. Remember that great strategies and tactics are nothing without continuous, relentless activity. So, once you have formed the strategies you plan to follow, work out what you need to do in terms of numbers.

Knowing the numbers

"To know and not to do is really not to know."
– Stephen Covey

Number of calls, emails, networking events, exhibitions, video posts, blog posts, podcasts episodes... These are your activity KPIs. Your aim should not be to set the biggest number, but to set the biggest number you can keep up for the longest time. Set monthly and weekly activity targets and stick with them, don't look for excuses and reasons not to achieve the activity targets – there should be none. You might miss your performance and sales targets for reasons outside your control. But there is no reason you should miss your activity targets. You are not in control of the output, not always at least, but you are almost always in control of your input.

Don't hide behind emails either. There is a place for emails and LinkedIn InMails. There's even a place for hard copy letters. But don't use these as a way to avoid real human contact. Calls and face-to-face networking are vital. They are harder to do, which is why they work so damn well: most of your competitors are shit scared of doing them, period. Get on it. The fear of rejection, fear of looking stupid or whatever it is that you're scared of, will go away the moment you get into calls and networking. The absolute hardest thing to do at networking events is to say "hello". Once you've done that, the conversation will take off by itself. The hardest thing to do with calls is to dial the number. It might take some time for you to get comfortable with it, but eventually you will make these calls and have these meetings a lot more easily and effectively.

There's nothing stupid about wanting to grow your business, and, if done right, cold calling and networking can make you look like a badass businessperson. If you really hate it, then make it one of your goals to grow fast enough so you can hire someone who does the prospecting for you. And do you know what the best way to grow quickly so you can find someone who does the calls and networking for you is? You fucking guessed it: do loads of calls and networking. Start now! Later on in this chapter, we'll talk in detail about cold-calling and networking. Use that to get some pointers and then get down to doing loads of activities. Sales and marketing are always about finding creative and effective ways to do an activity and stick with the grind – do, do, do. Activity is king. Bow to activity.

Actions

- Ensure you or your business development team have a rock-solid mindset about selling. If you have done the best pitches you possibly could, 'no's are okay – they are only a step toward the 'yes'. Ensure your team feel comfortable with 'no's.

- No 'maybe's.

- Measure activity and results from the start. It's a numbers game, always. Start tracking outcomes and KPIs so you can form a clear picture of your metrics.

- Once you have confidence in your plan, focus on your activity – the outcome is only a product of that. It's a bit like sport: the outcome, the final result, is the result of the activity. If athletes focus on playing well, the scores take care of themselves.

THE MARKETING
ON LINKEDIN

LinkedIn is an incredible platform, but it was many years until I started using it the way I do today – way more strategically and, I think, more correctly. If you are growing an agency, or any business really, LinkedIn is an incredible tool which provides big business development, branding and networking opportunities, mostly because it's super untapped. There are a few elements that will allow you to succeed on LinkedIn, and before you skip to the next part, either because you think you know this already or because you think LinkedIn "isn't for you", stop. I had similar feelings until just over a year ago. Do us both a favour, read the whole chapter and then decide. I'm limiting the LinkedIn strategies I'm sharing to the very few that I know can work to grow your business. You could write an entire book about LinkedIn, and many people have done that, so I won't. I work with the 80/20 rule: I've included here the 20 percent of strategies that are likely to get you 80 percent of the results. These are:

- Profile
- Be human
- Content
- Relationships

- InMails

Profile

LinkedIn is a professional network, so you want to look professional – leave that photo where you have a pint in your hand and you look a little bit 'happy' on Facebook, if you really have to use it somewhere. Use a professional headshot for LinkedIn. That doesn't mean you have to be suited up, it just means that you have to look professional. If you are the kind of person who goes to the office wearing geeky t-shirts, then just wear that kind of stuff. Be the you who shows up to meetings and to the office.

Use a neutral or office background – it will look more aligned with the platform and your profile viewers' expectations. You might think this goes without saying, but the number of profile pictures I see where people are on the beach, in the pub or in some other unprofessional setting is still incredible. This isn't set in stone, there are exceptions where some 'lifestyle' pictures work. But most don't, and even when they do, they give you no advantage, only risks. Want to stand out? A flat background photoshopped to be a bright colour might work if you believe that being noticed in the news feed is important. For the strategies that we'll cover, it isn't.

Right now, I am experimenting with little graphics and emojis in my profile description and it seems to be going down well. I'm not talking about smiley faces, I'm more talking about things that represent graphs, little rockets if you sell, or whatever else that might add colour and fun, and help you stand out. If that's your thing, then go for it; if it isn't, then don't. I think the message here is to always have your profile as aligned as possible with who you are in real life. The bigger the divide between the real you and the LinkedIn version of you, the more you might have to fake it when you meet people in person.

At the moment, my LinkedIn profile reads:

"Director at Genie Goals ⁓ Google Award Winning Agency ⁓ Top 3% in EMEA ⁓ Buffalo of Digital Marketing ⁓ Google Speaker ⁓ Personal Development Self Proclaimed Master ⁓ Entrepreneur ⁓ Lover of Shoes and Odd Socks"

I'm experimenting with this and I've certainly seen no repercussions of its playfulness. I'll update it as times change. Your profile, in essence, just needs to say what you do and what you like. Are you going to put some people off by being totally you? By showing that you are a strong individual and have strong opinions? Yes, for sure. Are you going to put some people off by showing that you are the opposite – someone always open to questioning their own opinion and soft in your approach? Yes, most probably. You are going to put some people off irrespective. Be you. A vanilla profile might not work either, in case you were wondering. When you meet with people or when they see you on video, they'll see the discrepancy. Your Linkedin profile should resemble you as much as possible.

In your experience section, a very good approach to listing your experience is to include the 'what', 'how', and 'for whom'. The 'what' is what you do, the 'how' is how you do it differently, and 'for whom' is your target market. For example, if I say in my experience section that I'm director of Genie Goals, I would then include:

- the 'what': "Genie Goals is a retail-only digital marketing agency, Google award-winning, top 3 percent in the EMEA."

- the 'how': "We have built our own retail-specific tech that helps our retail specialists run campaigns in 13 native languages."

- the 'for whom': "Genie Goals operates strictly and exclusively in the retail sector, helping retail brands grow nationally and internationally, covering channels like paid social media, PPC search, affiliate and marketplaces."

Then you'd follow the same structure for any other roles that you might have. This is just one of many structured approaches to filling in your LinkedIn profile. Do you have a better one? Use that. You don't? Then use this.

Be human

Simon Bourne, founder and CEO of a brand called The Hand Dyed Shoe Company, built his successful business entirely on LinkedIn. When I say "built", I mean that from zero, he is now in House of Fraser, and his brand is loved, I mean really loved, by his customers. He is loved by his customers too. During an interview with Mark Williams on his LinkedInformed Podcast[1], Simon was asked how he managed to get into House of Fraser (because the House of Fraser buying department is renowned for being hard to win over), he said: "I don't know because they came to me."

The head Buyer at House of Fraser followed Simon on LinkedIn for about a year and then approached him. Simon has built a brand that is successful and desired, not only by consumers but also by department stores, and he's done all of that on LinkedIn, virtually for free. When Mark Williams asked him how he did it, Simon said that he opened up to his

---

1 http://linkedinformed.com/episode207/

network – he shared not only the stuff he did that made him happy and worked out, but also the stuff that didn't work. He opened up about his struggles, he showed his emotions. And guess what happened: people responded. They were supportive, they reached out offering help when help was needed, and they showed gratitude for Simon's openness, which was encouraging and relatable. People became raving fans. Couple that with his outstanding product, his WHAT, and his passion for what he does, his WHY, and you have a solid business built almost entirely by being human.

Content

As I write this, LinkedIn is still the best platform for professional content. LinkedIn has 500 million users, 250 million of whom are active monthly users[1], 40 percent of whom use the platform every day. What's more, LinkedIn is still growing: the number of users went from 470 million in 2016 to 500 million at the start of 2018, and counting.

This is the best place to show off your best work, add value and get credibility. You write articles and don't post them on LinkedIn? Mistake. You create video content and don't post it on LinkedIn because you think it's only for YouTube? Mistake. You record podcasts but don't post them on LinkedIn because you think they belong on Spotify or iTunes? Mistake. Got case studies? They should go on LinkedIn. Won a major account (or a small one)? Shout about it on LinkedIn. Have a webinar coming up? Post it… on LinkedIn.

Check out my LinkedIn profile at www.linkedin.com/in/lucasenatore/ and see what I post. Yes, many of the videos aren't polished, but they are out! Remember: sometimes you need

---

1 Q1 2018

to fix the plane as you fly it or, as my friend and best-selling author Rob Moore says it, right in the title of one of his books: *Start Now, Get Perfect Later.*[1]

Many people act as if they're scared of LinkedIn and only post content that's super-polished, amazingly professional and TV quality. Problem: it's six months too fucking late! They had the idea when something was topical and hot, but after six months the topic has cooled off and the beautiful piece of content is now irrelevant. What a waste. Other people might get stuff out a bit faster – after two months, maybe even one – but it's expensive and they put all their eggs onto that video basket (and one month is still slow... one week is slow for video content!).

The thing with content on LinkedIn, or any platform for that matter, is that you almost never know what will work and what won't. What will resonate and what won't. I have created pieces of content I thought were going to fly, go viral and get me hundreds of interested eyes. Wrong. At times I've had to check that content was actually live because it was getting zero attention, zero interaction, I mean none at all. Then I'd send out a piece of content that was good (I'd never send out something I don't feel passionate about), but perhaps extremely rough – shot in the car or as I walk Sofia, our boxer dog – and it would get traction as if I was paying people to interact (which, by the way, I don't).

We never know what will get a good uptake. If you spend a month and a few hundred, if not thousand, pounds creating a polished video, and then get no engagement, the disappointment of the low interaction burns on your skin like lemon juice on a papercut. Discouraged and broke, you say: "Fuck you, LinkedIn! Fuck you, videos!" But it's not their fault!

---

1 https://amzn.to/2GCCiIW

Now imagine this. You listen to this crazy Italian, and instead of sending out polished, perfect videos, you start sending out 80/20 videos – videos that are only 80 percent of the quality they could be but cost you 20 percent of the time and money. You post two a week – yes, I said two per week, not per month. I can post one a day on a roll, so you can definitely do two a week. You spend at the very most 15 minutes per video recording and 30 minutes editing. So you have spent 90 minutes a week, and you've spent zero pounds. Do this for 11 weeks (one quarter with one week's holiday) and you will have invested 16.5 hours, zero pounds and have 22 pieces of video content on LinkedIn. For no extra investment, apart from the time it takes to upload them (which you could use a freelancer for), you could post the same content on various platforms: YouTube, Facebook, Instagram, Twitter, Vero and more. You could ask a member of your team, or pay a freelancer, to adapt the length of the videos to suit each of the platforms. You could also get them to create voice versions of the videos and turn them into podcasts. Finally, get them transcribed (a great tool for this in the THE TOOLS chapter later on) and you'll have 22 articles. So in 16.5 hours over a period of 11 weeks, you will have produced:

- 22 videos on several platforms

- 22 podcasts

- 22-66 soundbite-type videos or text cut and edited from the full version (not by you – so no time needed)

- 22 articles

If you use one video, one podcast, one article, one soundbite video and one soundbite text post every week, you have more than five months covered posting daily. Get someone to build a posting calendar for you so that don't use the same content in the same week, for example:

Week one:

- Post full video A
- Soundbite version of video B
- Soundbite version of article C
- Full article D
- Podcast E

Week two:

- Post full video B
- Soundbite version of video C
- Soundbite version of article D
- Full article E
- Podcast A

And so on.

With that amount of content, you have a much better chance of getting traction and seeing what works. Now you have a real opportunity to see what resonates and what you need to do more or less of. Some people will engage with written content and totally reject the same content in a different format. This way you'll get to see what's what. And it took virtually nothing to produce it all – 16.5 hours. Sound like a lot? It's not. Later, in THE PRODUCTIVITY chapter, we'll look at how to get more from your working hour. But for now, if you're honest with yourself, you waste more time than that. Look at the last three months and honestly answer these questions:

- How many of the meetings I had were necessary? How many hours have I spent in meetings that could have been avoided?

- How many one-hour meetings could have been done in 30 minutes or less?

- How much time have I spent browsing Facebook or LinkedIn?

- How much time have I spent doing tasks that could have been done by someone else but that I wanted to do because I'm a control freak?

I bet that if you're honest with yourself, you'll easily come up with more than the 16.5 hours you need to get this content out. Content is always king. What will change over time is the quality of the content: people want more and better content, and by better I mean more inherently good, more informative, more entertaining, more useful. I don't mean more polished. LinkedIn has changed and is no longer the CV, job hunting, recruiters' mecca it used to be. At least it's not just that. Now LinkedIn is a place where you can win if you post good, relevant and real content. Get on it.

Network

Celebrity entrepreneur Gary Vaynerchuk's well-used phrases "you need to add value first", and "jab, jab, jab, right hook" are key here. "Jab, jab, jab" stands for give something for free – give something valuable first, a soft call to action, a link to a good video, good content that is genuinely valuable to the reader. The "right hook" is you asking for the sale.

The concept is very simple but important; it's been around for ages and many books describe it in different ways. You'd think it would be common knowledge by now, but we're still buying books about it, and we still react as if we just discovered hot water for the first time. Then give it a few weeks and most people go back to the "buy, buy, buy", and "must sell to you right now" approach. There's clearly a lack of patience epidemic. I am passionate about this because I believe it is vital. In order for people to trust me, in order for people to buy from me, in order for people to be excited about what I do, I must show value first. Especially now that we are in the era where choice is virtually infinite and easily accessible. We must show value before we sell.

That's when content helps. We'll come back to that; first let's touch briefly on your network. You need to build your network of contacts and establish relationships with them, because if you don't, who's going to consume your content?

If you don't have an extensive network of contacts on LinkedIn, you need to grow one. If you have a good network of contacts on LinkedIn, you still need to grow it. I don't have a big network, around 4,000 people at the time of writing, and I'm working to grow it – I'll share how I'm doing that shortly. I'm assuming that you add every single person you know, everyone you meet in person, and everyone you're connected to in other networks. I take that for granted. You don't? Start doing it. It's crazy not to. I've won business that I can directly attribute to having done this. Do it.

I have added loads of people with the title Head of E-Commerce, sending them a personalised message talking about e-commerce in the connection request (you only have 300 characters here so be concise). I typically write: "*Hello NAME, always great to connect with people in the same field, especially one as fast-moving as FIELD. I look forward to exchanging insights and ideas on here and perhaps meeting in person at one of the many UK events. Have a great day ahead.*" If I know they are based in a specific city or town, then I replace UK with their city. Works great.

I did the same with people whose title was E-Commerce Manager, E-Commerce Director, and any variation of these or similar roles. Then I replaced E-Commerce with Digital Marketing, so I searched for Digital Marketing Manager, Head of Digital Marketing, Digital Marketing Director and so on. I did the same with Acquisition Marketing, Performance Marketing and other relevant titles. You can take the same approach to adding people in your target market. The list of people you are able to add using this method is gigantic; you're not deceiving anyone, you're not selling to anyone and you're adding people who should be glad to have you in their network. Why? Because if you don't sell hard to them and you post good content, as we've talked about, they are in for a sweet treat: a decent amount of content from someone who knows their stuff in their field.

The key here is: do not sell. Do not sell. Absolutely do not sell to the people you add. Even when they accept, even if they reply to your note saying how glad they are that you added them, do not sell to them unless they say something like: "we were just looking to get proposals from... are you interested?" Unless they ask directly, don't destroy their trust in you, in the industry and in LinkedIn by selling to them. That would really be terrible.

But if you add relevant contacts with an intro note that 'converts', your network will grow massively and very quickly.

And you don't just look for prospective customers or partners. For example, if I was running an agency that does paid media, I would probably add PR agencies. I would probably add anybody in advertising, design or retail, or anything that is in some way relatable. I aim to invite 100 people each week, which ends up being 30 new contacts in a bad week and 60 in a good one. I fail at keeping this up every week, I probably average two weeks per month. That's enough.

Remember, you are not selling, you're looking to build relationships. You don't yet know what these can give you, but you know they'll give you something. Sometimes it's a new contact who you might become friends with, sometimes it's a new contact who just shares something useful and sometimes it might be someone who goes on to refer you on to their customers because you offer something they don't, and you built a relationship in which they trusted you.

I think you have one burning question:

"Luca, how the hell am I going to find the time to invite 100 contacts a week to be able to add 30/60 people per week?" (Conversion might vary depending on your message.)

There's a tool in the section THE TOOLS for this, which allows me to invite 100 contacts in about three minutes.

Relationships

At the time of writing, what dictates the ranking and the popularity of posts is the engagement rate, likes and comments more than shares. The more people comment and like the post, then the more people will see that post, because people in their network will see that they have engaged with it. You should absolutely encourage commenting and likes on your posts, and reply to comments with questions so there will be more comments. All of this needs to be natural and sensible

– don't try to drag the conversation on just for the sake of ranking, that's silly. But if you post something and someone comments saying: "that's so true, I can relate", replying to that comment with "Glad you agree, NAME. Something similar happened to you?" is perfectly fine. This is how people would interact in person, so why not do the same on LinkedIn? If the conversation has naturally come to an end, then that's it, you move on.

You are more likely to promote engagement by asking questions. Even if you just post that you won an award: "I am so excited all that hard work paid off! We won an award with organisation X and I'm chuffed because this has been the direct result of hard work. I'm sure you can relate, what have you achieved that you could directly attribute to hard work? Hearing stories from other people inspires me more than reading my own, so come on, share!"

You're asking a question, you are eliciting answers and facilitating a conversation. Compare that with just: "I am so excited that hard work paid off! We won an award with organisation X and I'm chuffed because this has been the direct result of hard work." You would probably get engagement with this, but nothing like the amount you would get by asking a question. I've tried, many times.

Another example could be when you hire: "We're hiring for a head of business development. Do you guys have any tips as to what worked well for you in hiring? Anything from any agency that you might have used, any interview questions that you thought were particularly useful? Any help, much appreciated." You're likely to get an incredible amount of interaction if you post stuff like that. The information you get can help you and everyone else who reads the answers, and your followers will absolutely love the fact that you're asking them to help. People love to help.

Have you recorded a video on how communication is important? Post it and say:

"We lost a client a while back because we just didn't understand well enough what they were trying to achieve with one specific campaign. We were still 'young'. I became obsessed with communication and yesterday, for some reason, that episode came to mind, so I decided to record this video for our staff and myself, as a reminder to always communicate well. What do you think?"

This shows that you are human, that you don't just brag, you admit to your mistakes. It gets people curious, making them want to watch the video. And you will get interaction, I promise. It's so much better than saying: "Here is the fantastic video on communication I did. Enjoy."

Start a conversation, ask a question, ask for help. As you're probably beginning to see, at the core of this whole theory, the principle is very simple, and it goes back to being human. Humans – the good ones at least – speak and act a certain way; they don't go out and just vomit at people the stuff they're going through, what they've got going and what they have achieved. Those who do tend to remain lonely – you see it in their posts, no one gives a shit. No one interacts.

Sometimes you may share a case study, a white-paper, a 'how to' video – "Five tips for winning more business", "Five ways to get the best out of Black Friday", "Five tips for growing a brand" – whatever it is that you have expertise in. Again, I would do that on LinkedIn, and ask a question if possible. You don't need to be perfect. Sometimes I post stuff without asking questions, either because I am testing, or because I simply forget, because I am human and humans forget. I am not perfect.

I tested some sections of this book on LinkedIn – I just put them out there in their raw form to see how people took them. I didn't always ask for feedback or pose questions. People's engagement (or lack of it), their comments and questions helped me shape my work. Many of the parts that I shared seemed to really resonate with people, which is a great way of promoting my book even before it's out – I was creating a buzz. The point here is you don't have to be perfect 100 percent of the time, just be aware of what is likely to work best and keep that in mind. If you only get it perfect 50 percent of the time, that's a good start. Now aim for 75 percent and keep moving.

Be out there – not only the CEO, the marketing manager, or the face of the business, but all members of the team should do the same. Give the people a face, and you give the brand a personality; give it many personalities by introducing several of your team members. What do they like? Do they have an interesting story? That's the type of content I'm talking about – engaging, real content that adds value and starts conversations.

"Do you guys find that you could improve your new customer acquisition process? I had this challenge for a long time, that's why I decided to do a video about the three things that worked for us. I'm aware there's a lot more that we need to do, so I'm so curious to understand what it is that you're doing that works for you. Maybe next time I'll do a video with those tips included too. These are tips that I know worked for me, let me know what has worked for you."

Post from your personal profile, not your company page. People don't want content from brands, at least at the time of writing. I keep saying "at the time of writing", by the way, because the landscape changes all the time. These things may have changed by the time you read this book. But the principles will probably never change; most of the marketing principles I have success with today are the same as the ones I had success with 20 years ago. Don't get hung up on the specifics of what you're reading but get absolutely obsessed with the principles.

Company pages on LinkedIn don't work. Nobody engages with them, nobody wants to see them. There is a place for them on LinkedIn – they're good for branding, good for recruiting and good for sharing information that's useful to see on LinkedIn, again, mainly for recruitment and credibility. So sure, post from your company pages about social events, awards, new customers, case studies, etc. But the real content, the conversation starters, the valuable content needs to be distributed from your personal profile, because people like to talk to people more than they like to talk to companies.

Don't just post on your profile, also comment on and like other posts. Add value. If you find something valuable, something you agree with, something you like, comment on it, like it and share it. Tag other people you know and say things like: "Hey, TAGGED CONTACT, check this post. I think it makes so much sense and I thought you'd like it too." As always, only do stuff like this because you genuinely believe it – don't be fake, it'll show. Don't have a hidden agenda, it'll show. To be clear, interacting with other posts hoping that you'll gain something out of it in the future isn't having a hidden agenda, it's good business. You are adding value to the conversation, helping the post author rank higher with that post by showing up and bringing your contacts too. If you are sincere in your words and comments, you cannot think of it as having a hidden agenda. It's is very transparent – you are on a professional network, networking, bringing value whilst giving yourself the opportunity to be noticed.

On the other hand, if you comment on posts directing people to your profile, your website or your blog, then yes, you've got a hidden agenda and that's not good. Of course, if you don't need anything from LinkedIn you might not do any of this. But if that was the case, you probably wouldn't be working on the platform in the first place.

So now that we've cleared that up, invest some time adding value to posts you like. If you like what's been published, say it – comment and like. Is it worthy of a share? Share it. This in turn will allow you to be noticed and expand your network of new contacts who might start interacting with you. That process is called building relationships, and this is the very beginning of it.

I sometimes share good content in a Facebook group for digital agencies. I've had several members of that group reach out to me to tell me they like the posts, they've added me on Facebook and Linkedin, and some have become penfriends. One of these is the group owner! If you add value, people will accept you, for the most part. Some might not, but if you do things right, if you are ethically sound about this, then it's most likely be their own insecurities driving their malcontent.

Frequency

There is an incredible amount of misunderstanding as to how frequently one should post on social media and Linkedin specifically. Daily? Weekly? Five times a day? Ten times a day? The answer is that it doesn't matter. What's more important is consistency, and even then, this isn't anywhere near as important as some might think.

If you post five times a day, then you should try to post about five times a day every day. But if you post three times on one day and six times another day, that's fine, even though one is double the other. The principle is that you've posted a lot on both days – three posts or six posts, that's both a lot. To be consistent, you simply keep posting a lot. If you post three times a week, then

151

try to post three times a week every week. And again, if it's twice one week and four or five times another week, you're still posting relatively little, so you're being consistent.

But what's best? A lot or little? Read ten books and you will find ten different answers. In my experience, a lot is better but **only if your content is always good**. This is extremely hard to achieve, because inevitably, some pieces of your content will be a lot better than others – richer and more useful. The danger of posting a lot – daily or multiple times per day – with content of variable quality or importance is that your audience might miss the good stuff. Being unable to consume everything that you post, they will have to choose what to consume and therefore might miss the high value content if they can't tell the difference before they engage with it.

If this is you, one way to go about avoiding the risk of your high value posts going unnoticed is to brand the richer content in a certain way so that you make it easier for your audience to distinguish the skinny daily posts from the chunky ones. I did that and it works very well. If you don't do this, it's possible that you'll lose the interest of your followers altogether.

The only situation I can think of in which you should be regimented in your posts is if you have some sort of show that you said will be published regularly, at a certain time on a certain day. If you do that, then you have to be consistent because you've set the expectation. I have tried to do that before and failed. I started a show giving out good-quality video content – interviews with people and other types of insightful and useful content. I allowed travelling and everything else to get in the way and stopped treating it seriously. Now I publish these richer posts sporadically. That's why the subscribers of the YouTube channel I'd set up for that show never grew. I will get back to it, but for now it's just not my priority.

One benefit of posting as close as possible to a regular time or day is that you'll form the habit of posting, which will help ensure you make the time to do it. This is the only really important reason for posting regularly, at the same time if daily, or day if weekly. In the agency business, I have seen no evidence of other 'side effects' of posting little or infrequently. What's way more important than frequency and regularity – many, many times more important – is *what* you post. The quality and nature of your posts.

Put the time aside

Another topic where people lose their shit. Posting regularly and well doesn't need to take much time. It takes me 10 minutes a day, probably three days a week when I post infrequently, and maximum 20 or 30 minutes a day, five days a week when I'm in 'content producing beast mode'.

Park 10, 20, or 30 minutes per day at the same time and get it done. Struggling with that? THE PRODUCTIVITY chapter ahead might help.

We've reached the end of the LinkedIn section. We've gone through a lot, so you might want to dive back in to different parts of it as you take action.

Actions

- Build a good profile. Take your time and look at other people who you follow. Compare their profiles to yours and to the 'guidelines' we looked at in the Profile section of this chapter.

- Be you. Post as a human, not as a JOB TITLE.

- Work on content. Produce as much content as you can.

153

You're not only a design agency, you must be your own media agency. You're not only a PPC agency, you must be your own media agency. SEO, CRO, Dev, Recruitment agency, you all must also be your own media agencies. Put time aside for this. Reread the 'Content' section and build your schedule.

- Give yourself a weekly target of people to add.

- Give yourself a daily target of posts to interact with.

- Take time out, plan for it, every week to build relationships on LinkedIn. Comment, like, share, interact.

THE MARKETING ON FACEBOOK AND INSTAGRAM

I absolutely love Facebook and Instagram as marketing platforms. I love them as a marketer, I love them as an agency lead and I freaking love them as a user to be marketed to! If used correctly, marketers have a real opportunity to serve content to very targeted users who want to see their ads. It just needs to be done correctly and sensibly, with the user in mind. All marketing channels should be treated in this way, and respecting this rule on social media channels is even more important, because these channels are unforgiving. Nobody is safe, even large brands. Especially large brands, in fact.

This isn't a book designed to help marketers use social channels better, if it was, I'd go on for absolutely ages about targeting, messaging, permission marketing, etc. If it was, I'd have asked my colleague and friend Simon Jared to write this chapter and he'd probably have told you the same. But just know this: **if you are aware and respectful of what users are trying to do on these channels, and adjust your activity, message and tone accordingly, you have strong chances of winning. If you don't, you'll become the Toys"R"Us of the advertising world.**

For agencies wanting to use Facebook and Instagram to market themselves, there are a number of good steps to take to do it well and effectively.

Real work

The first one is to start doing real work on these platforms. What I see now is agencies being on social channels the way most others are – the way that's vanilla, the way that's safe. Fuck safe! Safe will not get you anywhere. Yes, maybe you won't piss people off, but you won't add value either, because guess what, almost everyone else does safe. There are some organisations that get it right, and they are winning. Who are they? You know this better than me. Look at your Facebook and Instagram accounts; which organisations do you follow and enjoy following, that many others do too, and that get loads of interaction? What do they do? These could be massive organisations or smaller ones. You are looking for those that get the results you want.

Find them and then be *like* them, but don't try to *be* them. Be you. What I mean by "be like them" is be as bold, as creative, as active, as able to experiment and as good at being part of the ecosystem as they are, but with your own flair, your own personality. These are the Gino Di Campos, the Graham Nortons, the Gordon Ramsays of modern business – these that are able to be themselves fully, and bring fresh energy to their environment.

I think your agency should absolutely be represented on a Facebook page, but your personal brand should lead. The reason is very simple: Facebook is a people platform. This may change, but right now, people like to see people on Facebook, and that's why I lead with my face. Can you have your company page push employees' content? Of course. Will it work as well? No. If each team member pushes out content related to your business and industry but through their personal page, it will get noticed more and by more people.

Here's how I'd do it: I would get every single employee to open a NAME @ AGENCY X page – Luisa @ Genie, for example. Then have Luisa, and every other employee, post at least once a day on their page. Some of the posts might be sharing useful or flattering content, tagging brands that you'd like to work with. For example, your employees might share the news when a brand wins an award, starts a relationship with a new brand ambassador, or gets a new CEO. From my personal page, I once shared a picture of me talking at Google with some amazing Gucinari shoes on and tagged the brand and Genie Goals. The brand shared the post on their timeline. All the Gucinari followers saw "Gucinari shared Luca Senatore's post" which had Genie Goals tagged in. And you know who follows Gucinari's page? Gucinari's customers, yes, but also Gucinari's employees, including the marketing manager in charge of selecting agencies. Watch this space :).

Imagine that was Luisa @ AGENCY X, and imagine it happened even just once a month with different brands. Imagine if every single one of Luisa's colleagues did the same. Chances are that the brands would sooner or later check out what on earth AGENCY X was. Imagine that you organise a free event for organisations in your target market, where you and other speakers share great information from different angles to solve a common problem your potential customers might be facing. Add some networking and food. You advertise this on Facebook, invite people and one of your customers clicks the 'Interested' button. All this person's friends will see: "Mike is interested in going to the Get Your Telecoms Site Ready for Q4 With Advanced SEO and Content Strategies. FREE Event'. There's a very good chance that your customer Mike has friends in the same industry but who are not (yet) your customers. See where I'm going with this?

Your employees will also share content you publish through your page and get your brand out a lot more than your marketing manager alone could ever do.

So don't sell on Facebook and Instagram, but post, be you, show your personality and get your staff to do the same. Flirt with brands you want to work with and use the company page as a portal rather than a content distributor. The content that works well on pages is company social events, recruitment, and announcements, including customer wins, awards, and so on. But the stuff that gets interaction, the interesting stuff where you can experiment and dare more, comes from you and the people in your organisation.

Facebook ads

I'm not going to talk about this in detail because it's pretty obvious. Advertising your agency on Facebook is a very good idea. Why?

- You can target Joe Smith, Marketing Manager at Brand X in North London! The targeting capabilities of Facebook allow you to target by location, interest, page likes and more.

- You could target people with an interest in digital marketing who work in the sector you are targeting.

- You could target people with an interest in SEO, who are in a sector you're targeting and who like the Google Analytics Facebook page.

The possibilities are almost endless, and, if the message is correct, you have a real opportunity to grow your brand awareness within your target market for next to nothing because (at least at the time of this writing) Facebook is dead cheap. You can buy video ads on Facebook for peanuts. I have reached 10,400 people with a video advert, having spent £19, and received 12.5K impressions; that's a £1.5 CPM on a platform where most of these would be on mobile, meaning my video would have taken up 80 percent, if not more, of their screen. That's crazy, and it's crazy not to do this.

£10 per day on Facebook can have a massive impact on your brand, but don't make the mistake of rushing into ROI and measurement. Focus on soft metrics: engagement, following, visits to blog, poll uptakes, etc. Don't get sucked in by obsessing about ROI. This will come. If you spend £300 per month on Facebook, even if it gives you one client every two years, you'll be in positive ROI (assuming you are able to keep your clients for at least two years once you win them and charge decent fees – they don't need to be boutique agency fees, just decent fees. More on fees later).

Get creative. Why not do a live stream when you or someone in your agency is talking at an event? Do a Facebook Live about a training you have going in-house. Or at a company social where you and your team are jumping crazily on a bouncy castle. Give your followers a tour of the office. Facebook Blueprint (https://www.facebook.com/blueprint) offers an incredible amount of information and training on how to use Facebook advertising products, including best practice, ad formats, strategist for tom, mid and bottom of the funnel and more.

Just like on Linkedin, be human. Follow the same advice you read in the Linkedin section. Be a person, it's easy.

Instagram

Instagram is pictures and videos, right? Wrong. Instagram is everything that pictures and videos can say, and they can both say a lot. Instagram can be a better communication tool than Facebook because on Instagram you have to get your absolute best content in one picture or 60-second video. As I write this, Instagram is about to launch the functionality to post longer videos – IGTV has landed – but its effectiveness and uptake are still uncertain. We shall see, I guess. But for the short, one-minute video, there's a lot that can be done. Those who nail this, those who are able to communicate inspiring and memorable messages through imagery and short videos, win. What this means is that creativity wins, not just large budgets. That's exciting because it means smaller organisations can beat the shit out of larger ones.

Did you just sign up a client in the fashion sector? Do they have a brand ambassador? Are their clothes worn by celebrities? Did they make a catwalk? These are amazing pictures you can post on Instagram, and with the right tags, they'll get you loads of eyeballs. If you're clever with your strategy, your client will share this with their audience, and guess what? Their audience is made of customers but also current and, importantly, former employees who might now work at a different brand and might notice you. Different brand = potential new client. Your new client's audience might also include their peers, similar brands in different sectors. Perhaps the picture you use is of a model who is wearing your client's dress and another brand's shoes. Tag the shoe brand too.

You see where I'm going with this? Specific strategy... No! I am not going down the tactics route, I am not telling you to do exactly this and I am not telling you this will work for sure. This might not even be possible – perhaps your client doesn't have brand ambassadors. Perhaps you can't get permission. What I am talking about here, I guess, is the type of thinking we need to engage in. To be really strategic. To really think outside the box. Be creative and be resourceful instead of waiting until you have the resources. Even if IGTV was to take off and kill YouTube, which it won't, the same applies. It isn't big budgets that win, at least not always. It's creativity, strategy, and being, you guessed it, human. Look at what humans do online; what do you do? You are trying to talk to humans, so being human in your approach to marketing your business is a good idea.

I get really frustrated when I consult with clients and I hear: "We don't have the assets. We don't have celebrities buying our stuff. We don't have the budget the large guys do." These are such bullshit excuses, and they're emerging through laziness in looking outside of what's already being done. Laziness in thinking outside the box, really outside the box, not just for the sake of it, but rather to find the best route to go from A to B. Lateral thinking. That's all you're trying to achieve. Stay focused on that and find clever ways to do stuff.

If we were face-to-face now, I'd dare you to give me any realistic situation that you perceive to be lacking resources and I'd bet you that I'd be able to launch a smart, low-cost campaign which would stand out and make sense. Would it work for sure? Would it drive loads of new customers? Maybe. But maybe not. The point here is that we would be launching something, and we would capture the attention of your target audience. It would certainly give us a good indication of what to focus on, and how to change what we were doing to get closer to the winning formula.

That's why I could dare you something like that, not because I think I'm great, but because I know it's not about winning from the offset. It's not about launching new creative campaigns that can win from day one. That's an illusion. It's all about being resourceful and trying stuff, testing in a control environment so you don't go bankrupt before you find what works. It's about taking calculated risks. If you give yourself permission to do this, permission to aim to launch rather than to always win, the pressure is lower and this allows you to launch stuff. **If you take some risks, you might fail and you might find winning strategies. If you do nothing, you will only fail.**

Sometimes the secret is to move away and stop looking at each platform from too close a standpoint. Step back and ask yourself: "How might we get the attention of my target audience on this platform? What do they look at? What do they follow? What are they interested in?"

There are plenty of books and courses on how to run Instagram campaigns; this book is not about strategies and tactics. These change all the time, and that's why you should always seek fresh, up-to-date information. Better still, get an in-house team and become leaders, become the experts in social media marketing, even if you don't sell it to your customers. Even if you are a creative agency or pure SEO or CRO, become social media experts and use this expertise to grow your business. It won't be long before you realise that you're good at it and therefore decide to offer it as a service, and that's fine. But first become the expert for your own business.

We did exactly that when we hired Simon Jared, an incredibly talented social media advertising professional who joined Genie to help us manage our social accounts. Within a year, he had launched a very successful paid social media branch, which we included in our proposition. Clients love him and his team, they love his work. I love him and his work too. What Simon brings isn't setting up the campaigns; my son Karlo, aged five, can learn that in a week. At 10 years old, my eldest, Maks, can do it already! Simon brings strategy, and real strategy is about creativity and lateral thinking.

The idea here is to be creative in your approach to business development and in your approach to everything. Explore all channels in an out-of-the-box manner, continuously asking yourself: **"What can we do that nobody else is doing?"** "How might we use this channel to add value for our target audience?" "How might we do the same thing in a different way?" These are the types of questions I think you should keep asking yourself. **It is very likely that the principles in this book, the channels and the concepts will be valid for a very long time, maybe forever.** What you need to adapt is your approach based on how these platforms evolve, how the users see them and use them, and how your business changes.

Test test test, experiment, and once you see something that resonates particularly well with your target audience, you can put some money behind it and use it as one of your bigger pieces – your hero content. The more you do this, the more hero content you'll find. When posts plateau, it's your sign to give them a break for a few weeks or months and then try them again, working on something new in the meantime. At times the old posts come back to life, and at other times they don't, in which case you just won't put money behind it but let them float.

Actions

- Work out who your target market is on Facebook and Instagram. Who do they follow? What are they interested in?

- Produce native content.

- Invest in Facebook and Instagram ads.

- Prepare a schedule for your posts using a tool like Hootsuite or similar.

- Explore Facebook Blueprint, a fantastic learning resource (https://www.facebook.com/blueprint).

THE MARKETING
ON GOOGLE

I couldn't possibly write this book without including Google. When it comes to promoting your business using Google, there are several advantages and useful tools that you can use. I'm going to focus on the things that are most likely to work for you as a digital agency. That doesn't just mean digital marketing agencies; if yours is a design agency, a creative agency, a branding agency, even a consultancy, the following can help you to use Google to promote your business and grow your brand.

Google's marketing powers

If you run an online advertising agency, what follows might be your bread and butter. It all might be stuff you already know well, stuff that you sell to your customers, even. If that's the case, read through it anyway, as it might offer some additional or alternative views. Or you might have additional views and points you can offer to me and the readers, in which case I'd love to hear from you. We might even publish them on the blog and send them to the book subscribers.

First, it's important to outline the powers of Google when it comes to marketing your business.

The first is reach: Google has massive reach. You can promote your business anywhere from your local town to the entire world. You can be in the UK and talk to somebody in South America. If you're selling your 'How to do SEO for telecommunication brands' video course, you can reach people all over the world easily. Reach is massive.

The second is cross-channel data: More and more people use Google products to live their lives – Gmail, Google Calendar, Google Maps, Google Photos, Google Drive, and so on. To use these products, users must be logged into their Google accounts, which allows Google to form a much more accurate picture of its users. This is good data. The aggregation and segmentation of this data allows Google marketing products to be the best in the world. I use Gmail, I use Google Calendar, I use Google Maps, I use Google Drive and Google Photos. Google knows a lot about me. They understand what I search for, what I do, when I do it and how I do it. I wake up in the morning and my phone tells me how long it'll take me to go to work. I love it.

For some people this is creepy, but for me this is just incredibly good. I want the providers to understand my habits so that I can be served information and advertising that is relevant to me. If you're not comfortable with that, Google allows you to choose and set your preferences in your account. Cross-channel is a massive advantage that Google offers because it allows advertisers to take advantage of its data across the Google products. Your adverts are likely to be served to the people who matter to you.

The third is performance: Google Ads allow you to do performance marketing. What I mean by that is that you have control, you might choose to only keep the campaigns live if they perform. You put them live today and see their performance today, or tomorrow at the latest. If the results aren't great, you can kill the stuff that doesn't work instantly, or move a few dials and see an impact on the performance virtually immediately. It's very flexible and test-friendly.

Let's look at the Google products you can use to promote your digital agency.

Google Ads

How do you use Google Ads if you're an agency?

Brand

I would always cover your brand. This means you pay to appear high in the Google search engine results page (SERP) when people search for your company name. Why? Even if when people type your brand name into search engines and the only company that comes up is yours, unless you come up with a very good and compelling result and presence, I would always recommend that you advertise on your brand terms. It costs you very little but it provides the users with a great experience.

Let's say that you offer web development and branding. You're called AGENCY X. If somebody types in "Agency X web development", then you are able to serve an ad about exactly what they were searching for – web development – because you have full control over the advert. If somebody types in "Agency X branding", then you're able to serve an ad that talks about branding. So, for very little money, you're providing a much better experience for your users because the quality of the message that you include in the advert is something that you can control 100 percent. Better ad copy = better experience. Better experience = better chances your customers will convert.

Generics

Do you want to win new customers? Then you can use Google Ads to advertise against generic searches. You pay to appear in a premium position within the SERP when people search for relevant keywords. For example, if somebody types into the Google search engine "web development agencies in Brighton", you can make sure they find you by paying for a high position in the results page with an advert that you control. Obviously, that's a more competitive environment, which is way more expensive than advertising on your brand name – Google Ads is an adverts auction, and costs are inflated when you compete with other web development agencies that are advertising and bidding on the same keywords.

You bid to appear high in the SERP, and the highest bidder, with the best quality score (QS) gets the highest position. The QS is, in very simple terms, a way to measure the advert that provides the user with the most relevant experience for the search they performed. This takes into account what keywords you are bidding on, the quality of the advert and the landing page you are directing the user to. The more relevant these are to each other, the higher the QS. The higher the QS and the bid, the higher the position. (Note that simply paying more won't get you the highest position, QS is important.)

It isn't necessarily the highest position that gets the best results. Some adverts might perform better at lower positions than they would at higher ones; that's why testing is important. It can get a little technical, but it's good to understand the mechanics of this, even if you use an external marketing agency or a freelancer. It pays off to know this stuff. Later in this section we'll explore how to maximize your results from generic Google Ads advertising so that you can make it work at a positive ROI.

When you advertise on Google Ads, when you pay money for your ads to appear, especially on generic keywords, the last thing you want to do is measure the performance just on sales. If you are in the service business, and especially if you sell high-ticket services like web development projects, which can reach £150K or more, then measuring the performance of advertising campaigns purely on the sales the campaigns drive is a very fragile strategy. Even if you sell £500-a-month services, relying on just the sale as a KPI is not a good idea. There are smaller steps that your campaigns help the users make, which can move them closer to the sale but not necessarily end in a sale on the day of the paid click. Some of these smaller steps can be measured as micro conversions.

Micro conversions are actions that users take on your site which are not a sale but move the users deeper into the funnel, closer to the sale. They could be things like a request for an audit, a request for more information, or a newsletter sign-up. It could be somebody interacting with your chat function or somebody visiting a specific page. You could call them leads, but thinking about them as micro conversions allows you to drive actions that might not necessarily be leads in the traditional sense of the word. Let's stick with micro conversions for this section.

Let's say that somebody searches for "branding agency in Brighton". They don't know you but they click on your ad. They visit a page and download a case study. That's a micro conversion because it takes them from not knowing you to having interacted with you, and now they've opened up a communication channel, they've moved closer to the sale.

The next step is to understand how much micro conversions like this are worth. The way that is calculated is simple: you work out how many of the people visiting the site convert to a micro conversion. So you are Agency X selling SEO services. Your average monthly gross profit per client is £500 and customers stay with you for 24 months, on average. That gives you a total lifetime value (LTV) of £12,000. Let's assume that for every

100 people you send to the website through a targeted Google Ads campaign, 5 percent download a case study, 10 percent sign up to the newsletter and 5 percent fill in the contact form. Let's then assume that these micro conversions convert to a full sale, respectively at 15 percent, 10 percent and 20 percent. So:

- for every 100 case study downloads you get 15 sales

- for every 100 newsletter sign-ups you get 10 sales

- for every 100 people who fill in the contact form you get 20 sales

This calculation tells you exactly what each micro conversion is worth to you:

- Each case study download: 0.15 sales

- Each newsletter sign-up: 0.1 sales

- Each contact form completed: 0.2 sales

The last step is to work in your margins. If you have a 50 percent margin, meaning that for every monthly payment of £500 your net profit is £250, you multiply that by the length of time your customers stay with you, which is 24 months – that's a net LTV of £6K (£250 x 24). That's your break-even point. If you spend more than £6K acquiring a new customer, you'll be at loss.

Let's imagine you choose to invest 50 percent of your net LTV on acquiring the new customer. In that case you'd have £3K at your disposal. Invest more than 50 percent and you're likely to get a higher volume at a lower margin; invest less and you're likely to make more money per sale but fewer sales. The hunt for the sweet spot begins.

In table 1, you can see this scenario in numbers. I've included

170

the website conversion rate (CR) to micro conversion. This is the percentage of website visits that convert into micro conversions. It tells you how many clicks you need to the website in order to drive these micro conversions, and in turn, it tells you what your maximum cost per click (CPC) needs to be. (I've chosen these numbers for ease of calculation; actual performance obviously varies depending on the individual scenario.)

Table 1

Micro Conversion (MC)	CR (MC to a sale)	Net LTV at 50% margin	Site CR (from click to MC)	Clicks required	Max CPC
Case Study Download	15%	£450	5%	**150**	£3
Newsletter Signup	10%	£300	10%	**100**	£3
Contact Form	20%	£600	5%	**100**	£6

To get to a situation where you have this sort of control, you need data. That's the mecca for any advertiser. Few get there easily. Many never get there. You need the highest level of confidence to base your budget on the LTV. If you do that, you win; your marketing budget will be bigger than your competitors' because you take a percentage of the total value of the customer rather than a percentage of just one month's retainer. This allows you to win more customers. These new customers might upscale their work with you and refer you to others.

Getting to that ideal scenario takes time and loads of data. The scenario outlined in the table is perfection – it's not easily attainable, but you can get close to it. The more data you drive, the more accurate your figures. If you do your job well – if you invest and collate data, if you measure the value of these micro conversions – in time, you will be able to set up a very precise marketing operation that you can rely on. At that stage, you will be king of your industry when it comes to running Google Ads.

But what do you do at the beginning when you don't have the data?

A more realistic scenario, at least at the beginning, is one in which you might not know how much an average customer pays you. You might not know how long they'll stay with you, or how your website converts visits to micro conversions and micro conversions into sales. When you don't know, when you don't have clarity or control over these KPIs, you have to invest. Speculate to accumulate, they say, and they are right.

At the beginning, you need to go on assumptions. You need to need to launch stuff, with small budgets, with good hypotheses and perhaps relying more (note I said more, not solely) on last click conversions, on sales. You might be more cautious with your micro conversions and only assign some arbitrary value to those which seem more likely to convert into sales. Things like contact forms and phone calls.

You have to accept a degree of guesswork at the beginning, but if you drive paid traffic to your site and you begin to measure micro conversions, LTV and the other metrics we looked at, you'll be ahead of 99 percent of people in your industry, I promise. Many don't do Google Ads at all because they can't be bothered. Yes, I said "because they can't be bothered".

Whenever they say "it doesn't work", whenever they say "it's not for me", what they really mean is "I can't be bothered to look into it well enough and make it work".

If done properly, Google Ads works for most people. The degree to which it works is different. The way in which it works is different. But it works for most businesses in the service space, and it works for most products. Not all, but most. Yet way too many people believe that they are in the 'doesn't work for me' group, for all the wrong reasons. We have made a lot of money at Genie Goals taking on brands others couldn't make work. We made them work, but not because we are better, not because we are smarter, not because we have more resources. **We made them work because we could be bothered, we gave a shit. We cared enough to work better and work harder. It's not genes, it's attitude.**

YouTube

YouTube is an incredible channel because it allows you to connect with people from within your target market when they are watching videos. Despite what you might hear about Instagram taking YouTube's audience with IGTV, people still watch YouTube when they have something in mind they want to watch. YouTube is a search engine, it's not a social channel the way Instagram is. I have the TED app, for example, but I usually watch TED talks on YouTube. I watch 'how to' videos on YouTube. The Joe Rogan Experience. Music concerts too. Sometimes, if I'm terribly bored, I watch news bloopers or 'Sacha Baron Cohen best clips'... all on YouTube.

YouTube has more than a billion users. 95 percent of advertisers would tell you YouTube doesn't work for advertising. Those 95 percent are *amateur* advertisers. Professional advertisers will tell you that YouTube works incredibly well, just not to drive immediate sales. YouTube works super well to drive brand uplift and generate brand awareness, direct eyeballs to your brand, get new customers and increase the share of voice your brand has.

Brand awareness

At the time of writing, only about 21 percent of the time people spend online is spent on Google search. The rest is spent elsewhere on the internet and on apps. By 2021, according to forecast published by Cisco[1], video will make up 82 percent of global traffic. What you do on YouTube is brand building, brand awareness. You build brand awareness so that people are more familiar with you and more likely to buy from you when the time comes for them to buy what you sell. On YouTube, you work at the top of the funnel.

- **Top of the funnel**: If you reach out to people who might not need to buy now but are in your target market, your audience is massive and you don't drive conversions. You are doing brand building.

- **Mid funnel**: If you reach out to people who are ready to buy but don't know you, the audience is bigger but conversions are lowest.

- **Low funnel**: If you only reach out to people who are ready to buy and know you, you are reaching out to a small audience and conversions are high.

- **Bottom of funnel**: If you only reach out to your customers when they need to buy again, your audience might be

---

1   https://www.cisco.com/c/en/us/solutions/service-provider/visual-networking-index-vni/index.html

small but conversions are highest.

On YouTube you can target people of certain demographics in certain locations. You can target people who are 'in the market' for your services, meaning that, according to Google data, these people have displayed behaviours that suggest that they might be getting closer to the purchase stage for what you sell. You can target 'similar audiences': people who are similar in behaviour and demographics to your current customers, and more. Advertising your video on YouTube is still relatively cheap, at least at the time of writing.

Engaging video content

You need to look at how to create effective video content which helps you grow your agency.

Rule #1: it needs to be engaging. There are very simple rules for creating engaging videos; here are a few:

- Start with the most exciting part. The most exciting statement. The attention grabber. Watch movie trailers to see what I mean – the explosions come first, the plot comes after. "Your website design is all wrong… I'll tell you why in a moment. Hi, I am John at Agency X. I looked at the 10 best website designs and the 10 worst, and what makes them so. See where yours sits. Keep watching." The shocker ("Your website design is all wrong") is the opener. The plot comes after.

- Drive emotions. Be funny, happy, ecstatic, sad and so on.

- Talk to the user. On TV, a video where the person is far from the camera and you see the whole body might work. Not on YouTube. Get close up, talk to the eyes.

These are just some simple tips that will help make your videos more effective. Get in touch with Google – ask them, they'll tell you. They want to sell videos because they want to grow the video platform even more. To sell video ads, they need people like you to create videos. They'd be very happy to share with you what works. As I write this, there are some interesting features in the YouTube Creator Studio. Explore that, do some research on YouTube itself, reach out to Google and you will know how to create good YouTube videos.

What content?

The type of content you might want to create includes:

- How-to videos: Did you write a blog post on how to make sure a website URL structure is sound? Do a video on it. Are you a web design agency? Do a video on 'things to ask a web design agency during a pitch'. You sell branding? 'The 10 best rebrands of 2018' might go down well.

- Recruitment videos: Show people what it's like to work at Agency X.

- Curate stuff: You sell PPC and Google Ads, Bing, or Yandex just released a new feature? A platform redesign? Do a video about that and what you think.

- Do you sell to brands? Do a video like 'Four Tips to Manage Your Digital Agency – Plus Two Bonuses', I did this one here at home, in 30 minutes: https://youtu.be/1vzwKQszqKo.

These are just some ideas for long-format videos. What also works very well is short, six-second bumper ads. These are very short, non-skippable video ads that can be very powerful for brand awareness. The number one rule here, which really applies to all formats, is to ensure you put your logo and key message at the beginning. Do a YouTube search on 'best bumper ads' for inspiration.

Why would you even have just a six-second ad? It's very cheap. You can reach an incredible number of people for a very, very, very small cost per view. Your brand is appearing in front of many people and that can be very powerful if you target the right people. Those who believe they bought Nike shoes because they saw an advert yesterday are delusional. You buy Nike because they have marketed to you relentlessly for the past 40 years. The sale advert you saw yesterday was just the trigger. Adidas might have run the same advert, but you wouldn't even have seen it because you're sold on Nike, so that's where your attention goes. People who think they buy their Mercedes over BMW because Mercedes is better, or because they saw an ad yesterday, or because they've always bought Mercedes... it's nonsense. They buy Mercedes because the way the brand speaks is aligned with their values. The brand presents itself in a way that is aligned with what they like.

Years ago, the Alfa Romeo was a car that kept breaking, more than any other car, but it still sold. Why? Because the company spoke a certain language that appealed to a certain group of people, a large group. These were raving fans. With bumper ads, you're presenting your brand and your tone of voice in front of people repeatedly, which increases brand familiarity.

It reminds me of a time when I was just starting out in marketing in Italy. I remember signing up a campaign for 100,000 leaflets which were to be distributed locally. Imagine this: I am a keen young wannabe marketer, extremely excited about this 100,000-leaflet campaign.

I say to my manager: "Yes, 100,000 leaflets! We can reach

100,000 houses."

My manager looks at me and says: "No, we're not going to reach 100,000 houses. We're going to reach 33,334 houses."

"Why? We've got 100,000 leaflets!" I tell him, thinking he got his math wrong.

"Because we're going to send the same leaflet to the same house three times in a three-month period. The first time, they don't know who you are, so it's just rubbish. The second time, they know they've seen you somewhere but they don't know where. The third time, they're familiar with you. Some may even think they've done business with you. If we send the leaflet to one house once, it will just go in the bin. **If we send it three times, it will go in the bin three times but it will stay in their mind, perhaps at the back – that's the best place.**"

That's why it's important to advertise on YouTube. Get into people's minds, right at the back, that's the best place to be :).

Retargeting

Once you've driven people to your website, whether through a PPC ad, a YouTube ad or a paid social ad, you have then the opportunity to retarget those people. By installing a simple line of code on your site, you will be able to follow the IP address that visited your site.

Somebody visits your site today. Tomorrow, they're browsing on YouTube, and if you retarget them, you are able to direct your advertisement to them. Why would you want to do that? Because if somebody has already been on your site, they are probably closer to the brand than somebody who hasn't. You can also retarget people who have seen your video on YouTube when they go over to Google and search for relevant terms.

Let's say that somebody has seen your video "How to ensure your URL structure is sound" on YouTube. You can retarget them and choose to pay more when they search for "URL structure best practice" or "SEO agencies in LOCATION" or similar on the Google search engine. You can retarget them on Facebook. On LinkedIn, on the Google Display Network (GDN) and many other places. And that's why it's important to do retargeting – it gives you the ability to talk to people who might be more engaged with you, and you might choose to invest more to target these people when they are ready to buy.

Conclusion on Google Products & Advertising Platforms

I'm aware that this book might be read by many marketing experts, so for you guys, if all this is very easy, skip it. You might not need it, although I always like to read and hear about things I know – I find I always pick up something new. For those who are not familiar with Google Advertising Platforms, this section was a brief illustration of some of the opportunities they offer. Get in touch with an agency that specialises in your sector – not us, we only work with retail brands. Seek to speak to agencies with experience helping businesses like yours, or reach out to Google, they can also help. If you're stuck, reach out to me, I can refer you to some good agencies in the service space.

As is the case for this whole book, it isn't a matter of you copying and pasting anything; I'm not giving you exact strategies and techniques, I'm giving you the principles, the concepts. The strategy, the tactics and the techniques might all change. The platforms might change, the people might, and probably will, change. You will change, your product will change, your service will change. But the principles are likely to last for a really long time. Google offers an incredible amount of opportunity to market your agency successfully, don't let it slip. Blog posts are good, social media advertising and social media organic posting is great, and offline advertising is incredible, I'm a big fan. But the power of Google is almost limitless. Don't ignore it.

Actions

- Get help with setting up and/or managing your Google Ads. This can either be from someone internal or a freelancer or agency, depending on the size of the account – a freelancer can only do so much. There is a point (typically when budgets are higher than £5K/month) at which agencies provide a better ROI.

- Invest in your brand awareness with engaging content.

- Look at the YouTube Creator Academy for specific tips and courses on shooting content, best practice, reporting and more: https://bit.ly/2cxM6kg.

THE NETWORKING EVENTS

Face-to-face networking isn't dead. Face-to-face networking is still alive – and very, very useful.

Yes, of course, the digital era allows us to reach many people almost effortlessly. But the level of interaction, the level of empathy and understanding that you can achieve in face-to-face networking is far, far superior to anything you can do virtually.

Like any marketing channel, face-to-face networking is evolving, it's changing, and we have to change our approach and adapt if we want to succeed. There a few things that will allow you to be more successful, more easily.

Research

With face-to-face networking events becoming more popular as a business development tool, we find that many more organisations are getting in the space and hosting networking events. This means that the quality of these events sometimes can be diluted to lower than it used to be.

There's nothing you can't solve with a bit of research. I would stay away from small local events, like the Chamber of Commerce or other national franchises which organise networking events locally. Unless, of course, your target market is local businesses. These events are typically well-attended by coaches, construction companies, plumbers, electricians, coaches, lawyers, accountants, coaches, many coaches, designers, coaches, millions and millions of coaches, and similar sorts of businesses. If that's your target market, then local events are great. But if you are a digital agency, targeting larger brands with monthly budgets of £10K or more, then you are very unlikely to find these companies at local networking events. You might, but it's unlikely.

Try to attend networking events hosted by companies that target similar organisations as you do. If you sell into travel, telecoms and finance, try to attend events hosted by organisations that target those sectors, and there are many. Do you sell into the retail sector? The British Retail Consortium (BRC) does too. Go there. There are countless examples like this; research is your friend.

You also need to research the topics discussed. You need to make sure that the topic addressed at the event you're planning to attend is relevant to you and your target audience. For example, if you are selling to the retail sector and you attend a BRC event, you certainly are in the right place, but you might not be with the right people. If that particular event is about merchandising, for example, or buying, or anything that has little to do with marketing, you won't find anyone from the marketing department there. Not only will the people attending the event be from different departments, but they might not even understand what you're talking about. Often within large brands, people from different departments don't even talk to each other.

When they think of marketing, they might think of TV ads and posters in the Underground. When they hear 'PPC' they probably think 'PPI', and SEO to many of these people is black magic. So even if you have an incredible conversation with somebody from merchandising, your name may or may not get to the right people. It probably won't, but if it does and you sell

SEO, they might say they met Harry Potter if you're lucky, or Voldemort if you're not.

So try to attend events that address specific topics relevant to your business. Let's say, for example, that you sell SEO to the telecom market, and there is a specific event that addresses website user experience and conversion rates. Now that is very relevant to what you sell, but it isn't exactly what you sell. This is a perfect event for you, because you will find the right people, talking about a slightly different but very related topic.

When you start a conversation with somebody at the event and they inevitably ask you what you do, you can casually say something like: "I actually do SEO, so not directly related to this, but I come to these events, because I'm really interested in understanding better ways to improve user experience, so I can bring them back to our clients and offer more value to them that way. I just find that it's something that works really well and it's something that our customers love. You know when you can add extra value to your customers, it means a lot to them."

And that kind of answer can go so much further than "Oh hey, I'm John, I'm from the best SEO agency in the world and I work with some of the best brands in the world." The former answer goes a lot further and it can get your name in the right place. Which brings us to the second point.

What to do

What do you do when you are at networking events? How do you make the most of being there? Let's start with what not to do: selling. Looking at the last example, you're not really selling, you're just having a conversation. And all of a sudden, you've already described one of the ways you add value to the people who choose to work with you: you go out of your way to attend networking events to gather information outside of what you sell – and therefore are not paid for – to bring back added value to your clients. What does that say about you and your agency? If I am a brand I would certainly be impressed. And if I was looking for an SEO agency, I would most probably ask you to come in and pitch. If I wasn't looking for one, I would definitely keep your business card, remember you… if you followed up then we might even build a relationship.

So no selling is number one; have meaningful conversations instead. Try to understand what people's pain points are, so that even if you come home without any contacts, you come home with data. You return with an understanding of what the industry is seeking. What are they craving? What do they talk about? What are the buzzwords? And that can inform the strategy and investment decisions going forward?

What matters at networking events is that your company is present. The more you're present, the more familiar your brand will appear to relevant people. The more familiar people are with your brand, the more your company's name will be passed on from person to person.

That's happened to us in the past. I met with someone from a very large brand at a British Retail Consortium event about internationalization for retail brands. We had a meaningful conversation, kept in touch, connected on LinkedIn, and eventually I was introduced in person to the marketing manager, who we'll call Michelle, at another event. A few months later, at an exhibition, I bumped into Michelle and we got chatting. I learnt we both knew someone from a CRO agency. In the next few years, I met a few more people from the same brand at other events, and in the meanwhile, some of the people I had met before left, including Michelle and Tim, the MD.

Fast-forward five years and we received a phone call from

someone I'd ever met from the same brand. She was in charge of e-commerce and digital marketing. They were looking for an agency to take over their PPC account, and she said that while she didn't know us, our name had been mentioned so many times in their office during the past few years that it seemed like they should absolutely invite us to pitch. We pitched, and between the pitch and the decision, our mutual friends at the CRO agency I mentioned before put in a massive good word about us. We won this exceptional global brand two years ago, and we're still going strong.

That's exactly what you're trying to create with your networking strategy. Be there, be nice, have conversations that are meaningful, and don't sell. Unless, of course, somebody tells you: "We need your services, please come and pitch."

Send your best people

The other element that will allow you to be more successful with networking events, is choosing who from your organisation to send to these events. It doesn't have to be you all of the time; it's better if it's not you all the time. Send your best people. Send your tech people, your creative team, the account managers. Tech people are always very impressive and so are the people who run the campaigns and accounts, the designers and the developers. Have you got a client services manager? Send her. Have you got a head of SEO or head of technical SEO or head of analytics? Send those people. They are very impressive and will represent your agency well.

But don't expect contacts and lists from them. We have seen this before: agencies send tech people to networking events with the expectation that they come back with contacts and leads. They won't, most of the time. Or they might, but they shouldn't be expected to. Most tech people are not business development people, and asking them to bring home leads is asking for them to do something that is not natural. Not only that, but it's also something they haven't chosen to do. They've chosen a technical career for a reason. If there's pressure to bring home leads, they might get put off from going to events in the future. If "becoming better at business development" is one of the goals you've agreed with them, then you might get away with it, though expecting leads isn't a good goal to set anyone, including business development people.

On the other side of the coin, there are agencies that never send tech people to these events because they think that tech people don't like networking. Most of the time, tech people don't like networking because networking is associated with selling. Send them to networking events that are relevant and where the content is useful for them. Encourage that and even the most introverted people will want to go because they are attracted by the content. They might meet people that are just outside of the role that you sell to, but if your tech people are impressive, they will build relationships with their peers and your company name will be passed around: "Heard you guys talking about needing a new agency for SEO. I met this woman at Brighton SEO, she seemed very impressive. I think she was from AGENCY X".

This stuff really happens, to those who put themselves out there. Invite your teams to go to events and not only do you get to network at more events without having to use all your time, but you also showcase different talents, different elements of your company. And you add value for your staff, because they get to get out and get good content.

Follow-ups

If you're attending networking events, you are likely to have three potential follow-up opportunities.

No follow-up: You met some people, you might have some business cards but there are no next steps. You just exchanged cards because it seemed like the right thing to do. I'd still add them on LinkedIn.

Good conversations: You met some people with whom you talked zero business and there is no obvious opportunity commercially, but you had incredible conversations. Maybe you talked about football or dancing, maybe you talked about education or family and holidays. You talked about everything but business. But you clicked. You hit it off, had a meaningful conversation and you exchanged cards on that basis. By "meaningful" I mean that you talked about something, anything, with true interest, fun and pleasure.

These are the people you should absolutely follow up with: "Hey John, it was great to meet you the other day. Interesting chat, really enjoyed it. Hope to bump into you again very soon. If there's anything I can do in the meantime, give me a call. Otherwise hopefully we'll meet soon. See ya, have a good day." It pretty much follows the same tone as your conversation had. If you had a personal conversation, don't start talking business in the email, because you'll break the rapport that you built. Simply extend the conversation you had, you will be surprised by the outcome. Obviously, you get to stay in touch with someone you got along with, and that's nice in itself, but also, John, the person you met, might be the person who overheard the SEO agency conversation in the previous example.

Stay in touch with John, send him a note now and again, whenever a good reason to do so comes up. "Hey John, since you and I were talking about education when we met at Brighton SEO I thought you might like this podcast. Let me know." Or maybe you haven't spoken with John in a few months and the same event that you met at comes up again, you could drop him an email: "Brighton SEO is coming up soon, can't believe it's been so long. Are you going? It would be good to catch up."

Things like this can go a long way, because John may not need your services now, but if you keep in touch in a positive way, following the same lines as the conversation you started, you are forming a relationship, and from there, opportunities arise. One day John might move to a different brand where they're in desperate need of SEO. Guess who John's going to call to pitch.

Approaching follow-ups this way costs you nothing and it can go a long, long way. You're not going to find many people with whom you hit it off like you did with John, maybe five or six in a given year. And to follow up with five or six people like that is only going to take you a few minutes each. A few minutes a year is not much time to invest, and the rewards can be amazing, on both a personal and professional level.

Business chat: You had a commercial conversation, you talked specifically about what you do, and John liked you very much, but they just appointed another agency. However, you both felt that there is an opportunity worth exploring in the future. Then I'm stating the obvious when I say that you must follow up promptly. "Hi John, great to meet you at Brighton SEO. I understand there's no opportunity now because you've signed a with another agency. But I'm excited to be talking to you, your plan is great and I love the brand. I'd love to explore opportunities in the future when the time is right, perhaps in six months or so, so the new agency has a chance to do their hopefully great job. Okay with me reaching out in five or six months?"

There is a fourth, but you don't need me to talk about that one, surely. Shit, can't resist: You met someone who told you they are desperate to get you in to pitch! If that happens... You got this. :)

As always, you need to kind of adapt these approaches to who you are. The point here, like I've said loads of times already, isn't to CTRL C and CTRL V what I say. It is rather to understand the principles and the concepts, get inspiration and ideas that are slightly out of the box and try stuff yourself.

Your own events

The vast majority of agencies will rely on going to third-party events, events organised by other people, events where you're supposedly going to find customers hungry to buy from you. The reality is that as the years have gone by, the ratio of suppliers to potential customers at these events has changed greatly in favour of suppliers – agencies. That means there are fewer potential customers and more peers and competitors. This makes it very difficult to invest in these events, because not only do you not know the kind of ROI that you're going to get, but it also just feels wrong. It's great to network with your peers and competitors, but not when your plans were to network with potential new customers. The expectation, the investment and the energy are misaligned.

The other problem with just relying on third-party events is that you rely on their way of doing it. Their content, their setup, their structure. You have very little control. If you organise your own event, you have control over the energy, the atmosphere, the content, the size, the duration, the freebies, the follow-ups and, crucially, the attendees' list. There's an incredible amount of opportunity in organising your own events. We have partnered with Google and we organise events at Google HQ. We invite a combination of existing customers and prospective ones. We provide useful, engaging, and practical content in a professional, inspiring and supportive, categorically non-salesy, environment.

Just a few weeks ago, we ran our second event with Google. It was all about the upcoming Q4 and Black Friday. If you're a retail brand selling online, Black Friday and Q4 are massive in terms of sales, and events like the one we organised can be really useful, if done well. We had a Google speaker and two speakers from Genie Goals, talking about topics including PPC, affiliate marketing, Facebook, YouTube, and Display. We had one of our customers sharing their experience and I was MCing the event. It was really inspirational, useful and practical content. No selling. No selling.

The last thing you want to be doing at these events is selling. You are there to provide good quality content, provide the delegates with an experience that lets them feel at home, where they can be surrounded by their peers and not by many other agencies trying to sell stuff. You can quickly see how the environment, how the energy of an event like this, can be very different from the energy of an event where there are more agencies than brands, and where the agencies chase an ROI because they paid to be there. Advertisers have their guards up. Advertisers have less bandwidth and mind space to listen, and it will be a very different dynamic compared to an event you run yourself.

At your event, you are giving, giving, giving and asking nothing in return – absolutely nothing. Your event is free, by the way. The effect that this approach has is that you create a space where everybody is together to collaborate, everybody is there to exchange information, there for the same shared objective, which is to succeed in business. Remember, jab, jab, jab, right hook. That's what you're doing here – it's a very long series of jabs. You're going to give an immense amount of value.

And building good relationships is all you're after. The rest will come, by itself. Trust the system.

If you can, try to partner with a large provider. We did this with Google. We have earned a good position with Google. We've won several Google awards and are amongst the very top agencies in the EMEA region. We got to where we are with Google not because of who we know, not by being nice, but because we perform well with our clients and win new business. Our retention is great, and retention is one of the things that Google looks at when building a relationship with an agency. If you retain your clients, then you're good. If your churn is too high, then there is a problem somewhere. Because of the growing size and the quality of our accounts, and because of the high scores in the quality of our accounts, we have been promoted within Google agency rankings several times, which means that we get higher support, a more comprehensive and experienced team of people at Google to assist us, and opportunities to do events like these.

However, you don't have to be one of the top agencies in your region for Google do events with you. There might be criteria and boxes you have to tick, but if you work well with Google, they'll work with you. I'm not saying they'd definitely agree to do events with you, that depends on your specific circumstances I guess, but they will support you way more than you might think they can. The same goes for any other provider you might be working with: Facebook, Awin, Adestra, Magento, etc.

When I give talks to agencies on behalf of Google, the vast majority I speak to don't take full advantage of their partnerships with Google. It's not a one-way street. We work with Google, we take the time to have shared business plans, we have meetings with them, calls, we check the health of our accounts, and we involve them in meetings with our customers.

191

It's a two-way street. Many of the agencies I speak to do none of these things. **Partnerships are like tandem bicycles; they can take you places but you both have to fucking pedal.**

If you don't work with Google because you're a design agency or a development agency, then find the equivalent. Are you a development agency? Ask Magento. Do an event in collaboration with Magento or Shopify. Do you sell paid social? Get Facebook involved. CRO? Optimizely. Email? Adestra, Pure 360. You get the idea. There are many organisations that you can partner with. Think outside the box, be creative. Once you sort things out and you are at your first event, remember, don't sell. I can't stress this enough. Don't try to sell at these events, or you will ruin them. Look to add value, that's all you're doing.

In terms of speakers, it works very well to have a representative of your business as the MC, so you can control the narrative and the energy. Certainly, one of the speakers ought to be somebody from the partner provider that you are doing the event with, whether that's Facebook, Magento, Shopify, Google or any other organisation – people love it and it's useful. Then have at least one brand that you've worked with that has had great success. The more known and successful that brand is, the better. That brand's job isn't to tell people how good a job you did, but just to tell a story, to get people to like that brand, what they did and what they are doing. If they can do that, people will start conversations with that brand. Guess who that brand is going to recommend when the question comes up: "Which agency would you recommend?" You could also invite another brand, one you don't yet work with, but want to. If you have one existing customer there, then inviting one you want to work with in the future might work very well. You can build a relationship with the potential new customer.

Pay attention to the speakers' styles and energy. Look for a good balance. Also, be sure to audio and video record your event, because you will use the recordings as marketing material going forward to promote new events.

Be generous. Giveaways, food, drinks... make it nice. Make it memorable. Make it remarkable.

Once the event is over, you should follow up with everybody. People have come to your event, the best thing that you can do is to send the slides, keep in touch, invite them to join your mailing list, and absolutely invite them to the next event. Certainly add everybody on LinkedIn, and then go back to the LinkedIn section of this book, and do what we talked about there.

Organising your own events in collaboration with some important players within your industry can really make a difference and can put you in a great place. It can place you next to large organisations like Google, Facebook, Magento, Shopify and many others. This helps you establish your agency as an authority in your space. Do it.

Actions

- Make a list of relevant events you can attend. Remember, be strategic about deciding what's relevant, think outside the box.

- Talk to your teams about networking and its importance and take away all possible concerns about performance. Reread the Send your best people section of this chapter if you need to remember what this means.

- Create a calendar of events you're looking to attend and decide in advance who from your teams is going.

- Create a way of tracking follow-ups, what's been said and what needs to be done next. Your CRM software is the tool for this.

- Contact some of your providers, peer agencies or clients and organise events together.

THE EXHIBITIONS
AND CONFERENCES

Partaking in exhibitions can be an incredibly effective way to win new business, but it has to be done right. If done incorrectly, it can be a very easy way to burn through your budget.

If you sell digital services, whether that's PPC, SEO, social media, design, development, or whatever else, then the events I go on to briefly describe below might be of interest. These have proven very effective for us at one stage or another. Obviously, depending on when you read this book, things might have changed. So whilst you may want to explore these specific events, it is more the common denominators of these events that you want to understand. What do they have in common? I'll give you a hand.

Types of Events

Internet Retailing Expo (IRX): Typically held in Birmingham, over two days, with anything between 10,000 and 20,000 attendees. Combination of talks in small workshop areas and large theatres. Many exhibitors.

E-Commerce Expo: Very similar to the IRX, but all about e-commerce, and typically held in London. The E-commerce Expo went through a bit of a change in 2016 or 2017. It used to be just e-commerce, and then it changed to the E-commerce and Technology for Marketing (TFM) Exhibition. After the transition there seemed as if there were a lot of startups and people working in the industry as freelancers, exploring the new technologies and networking. That might have been a coincidence, but we haven't gone back since.

Figaro Digital: A series of seminars and talks, typically in London, about SEO, paid search, or social media. We invested in this a few years ago because it put us in front of the right audience. Two things seemed to have happened since then that caused us to stop going: One, the focus seemed to have shifted more to SEO than paid marketing and we don't sell SEO. Two, the ratio between potential customers and agencies changed, and not in the way you'd want. By the time this book is out, this might have improved.

The eTailing Summit: Typically in London, with a focus on one-to-ones. There may be talks during the day, but the main stage for advertisers and solution providers is during the one-to-one meetings. Each pre-arranged meeting is based on the buyer's brief and the solution the provider is offering. Now this sounds like a dream. Buyers who want to buy and sellers who want to sell. Hit me! Unfortunately, it's not as good as it sounds, simply because the way in which they match buyers and solution providers isn't always based on a real brief. Sometimes, it feels as if the matching is done rather loosely. It's still a fantastic opportunity because there are great brands there, and if you are good at building relationships, I can see this type of events delivering massive ROI in time.

We did one of these four or five years ago for the first time and took the stage for a 10-minute talk. Normally, they'd charge anything between £2K and £3K for agencies to speak on stage. That time we got to talk for free because someone dropped out

196

last minute and they had to fill the slot. I took it. I spoke for 10 minutes and went home. The day after I got an email from one of the attendees, impressed by what we said, and asking us to pitch. They are still our customer today, and the person who got us to pitch has since moved to another global luxury brand; only last month, we won that account too. You work out the ROI of that event.

I've highlighted these four events because they represent the ones we tried; there are many in each category. Then you also have the conferences – Hero CONF, Brighton SEO, PILive, DMEXCO, etc. We don't have much experience there, we've done a little, but nothing I can write about. Make a list of the events you'd like to invest in, visit them as a delegate first if you can, and test. Some of the events we invest in have not yet given us an ROI, but we know that all it takes is one customer, then it pays for 10 years of events. As a whole, exhibiting at events in general has provided massive ROI for us so we don't measure it too strictly on individual events. We look at the category, in this case "exhibitions".

Approach to exhibiting

The most important thing is how you approach events, because you can be at the best event in the world, but if you don't do it right, you will get you zero out of it. I know, because I've been there, a few times. Then we learnt. So let's look at a few factors that are likely to give you a very positive experience and a very positive ROI.

Go all out: If you have a budget that barely covers the cost of renting the space, don't do it. Do something else, do it later or do something smaller. If the space costs you £7K, then you need to budget, at the very least, another £7K for everything else. You need to dress the stand, you need to get t-shirts for the staff, you need to get collateral, brochures, giveaways, and so many other elements. Costs pile up in no time at all. If you are on a small budget, you end up representing your agency very poorly because you spent all your money being there.

If you don't have the budget this year, do it next year. If you don't have the budget for the big one, do a smaller one. It's very important that whatever event you do, you go all out and represent your agency well. If you can't represent your agency well, who will ever trust you to represent theirs? If we look back at the way we presented our business a few years ago, we all feel we didn't do as good a job as we do today. That's natural. We didn't know what we didn't know. But if you don't represent your business well because of lack of funds, that a sin. At exhibitions, you need funds to represent your agency well.

Sponsor: If the event allows it, and most events do, I would definitely be a sponsor. If they've got a guide, make sure you're in it. If you can have your logo at the entrance, make sure you take that opportunity. If you can appear on their website during the build-up to the event, absolutely make sure that you pay for that.

These are all elements that will allow your presence at the event to go a lot further and produce the best results. It's the equivalent of doing advertising on just one channel versus doing it on PPC, on YouTube, on social media, on a billboard in the London Underground and through some leaflets. At exhibitions, make sure that you are everywhere. If you can afford to do that, it will greatly increase your chances of winning business. If you cannot afford the extravaganza, fine, do what you can. But remember, the bare minimum is:

- **A great-looking stand:** It's not about the size, it's the look and quality of the stand, which you get with good quality panels and furniture and creativity.

- **Enough staff:** Depending on the event, at least four. We usually have eight or more staff members.

- **Loads of giveaways:** Useful stuff, good quality. Notebooks, branded water, USBs, t-shirts, toys for kids, etc.

- **Collateral:** Good design. Good paper.

- **Drinks:** Money to pay for drinks at the after show party – that can get expensive.

- **Marketing:** A campaign before and after the event.

That's the minimum. Ideally, you want to add:

- More staff.

- Free drinks at your stand one hour before it ends.

- Sponsorship and marketing push from the event organisers before, during and after the event.

- A large inflatable thing outside in the vicinity.

- A speaking slot.

Pay to speak: There are normally conferences and workshops at exhibition events. Make sure that you have a slot to speak, if you can afford it. This can cost you anything between £1K and £3K, but it's worth every single penny because you get the opportunity to talk to anywhere between 20 and 200 potential customers about what it is that makes you good. And obviously, if you look back at the selling section of this book, you'll know that you're not gonna go in with the "we, we, we, we, we" speech. But you're going to go in adding value. You're going to impress. You're going to give people something that makes them go, "Wow! These people are good."

Giveaways: Don't go down the offensive route of giving away insignificant things that disrespect marketing and make your agency look really cheap. Give stuff that adds value: high-quality notebooks, with a personalized message inside, if you can. We give away water – we order loads of water with personalized labels that have our name on them, along with something interesting. When we were doing just PPC, we had a bottle of water that said, "You are 70% water. We are 100% PPC." That's a giveaway that adds value because people are thirsty, and water is important. Give away stuff that people can actually use and that will make them remember you. Go all out. You might spend twice as much as you normally would on giveaways, but people will keep them. There's no point in spending £1 a piece on something that will end up in the bin. Much better to spend £3 a piece if people keep it and use it. Funny giveaways are okay, but be careful, the line between funny and tacky is very thin.

Staff: You need to man the stand, and this contributes to the cost being higher. If you go to an exhibition, you want to have many people at the stand. One, it gives the impression that you are big and you're committed. And two, most importantly, it means you have time to speak to people. We have made this mistake before: if you only have a few people at the stand, then you might not have time to speak to everybody who comes along, which is a real pity because every conversation missed is an opportunity missed. Who of the people you couldn't speak to was going to be your £180K customer?

Build-up: If you book space at an exhibition event, you are likely to book it many months in advance. Make sure that you do a good build-up. Make sure you get in their newsletter, and when you do, give a ridiculous offer to the people who engage with you before the event. For example, let's say you sell SEO. You may offer a 100 percent free audit for people who sign up in your newsletter. And then make that same offer when you go out on the show's communication to their list. That way you can engage with people even before the event takes place. You could offer a one-to-one half-hour consultation at the event to anybody who books it during the build-up before the show.

Data: During the event, you must collect data, from everybody you talk to. Normally, you would get a scanner so you can scan people's badges or just get their email addresses and details so you can follow up. The follow up is vital. You will have a vast number of conversations with people, and it's important that you follow up. You follow up in a very consultative way, not being pushy. You certainly want to carry on building relationships after the event. If you fail to do that, a big chunk of your investment will have been wasted. Remember to make clear notes of who's who. I've made this mistake before – back in the office, I had tens of business cards and no clue what I'd said to whom or who they were. What a fuck up. Don't do it. Make clear, comprehensible notes with names and cues.

Patience: We had the first conversation with one particular brand at an event and ended up winning the business 17 months later. They became a customer, a good customer and went on to be worth £180K in gross profit to us over the course of three years. If we hadn't followed up and nurtured the relationship the way we did, we would've missed out on a great relationship with a great customer. We are still having conversations with people we met at events four and five years ago. And I can tell you, some of these contacts will become customers at some point in the future. They will stay with us for a long time, like all our customers, and spend £200K to £300K in their lifetime with us – and be happy about it, because we'll help them revolutionise their digital marketing. We'll help them grow massively so that the money they pay us means nothing. For that kind of money, for that kind of satisfaction, for that kind of growth, yours and that of your customers, you want to follow up, for as long as it takes. And you will.

You'll invest in marketing. You'll capture data. You'll follow up with prospective customers and you'll build relationships. Then you'll win business and you'll charge what you're worth. You'll grow massively, as you help your customers grow.

Actions

Choose the events you're going to exhibit at next year (or next semester if you're late in the planning) and get quotes. Negotiate – especially if you book early, you can negotiate heavily.

- Budget so you can go all-out, sponsor and take as much estate as you can comfortably afford to.

- Speak. Get in front of potential buyers and send them to your stand to extend the conversation.

- Be original and strategic about your giveaways, plan ahead and put real thought into this. It can make a massive difference.

- Decide early who's going to attend from your teams. Some exhibitions are two days or longer. Taking staff out might put strain on the workload. Plan ahead.

- Ensure you have a way of collecting data during the event.

- Prepare a follow-up campaign; this has to be ready way before the event.

THE COLD CALLING

(I KNOW YOU WANT TO SKIP. DON'T.)

Cold calling isn't for every organisation. In fact, many of the people reading this book might work at an organisation where cold calling is not ideal for acquiring new customers. Perhaps it's never been done and will never be done… in that way. Cold calling is misused, misinterpreted and misunderstood by most people, especially those who don't do it, closely followed by those who do it badly. Most people think of cold calling as a way to sell stuff to strangers. "Who gives a shit about them?! I just want to sell my stuff." Attitudes like that drive me insane. The second worst is: "I know them and I want them to buy my stuff. They will like it." Naivety and arrogance mixed in a bitter-tasting shake.

I invite you to think of cold calling as not selling.

You can use cold calling to invite people to your event – your free event. You can use it to do market research. You can use it to ask if they want the white paper on their industry you've just completed in collaboration with LARGE INDUSTRY ORGANISATION.

Cold calling is a relationship starter. Put it this way: You're out on a Friday night. You see a person you fancy. You approach the person and say: "Let's go sleep together. Fancy that?" What response do you expect? This is the equivalent of looking for a sale on a cold call (for the type of business this book is written for, at least). Instead of going in for the kill, talk about the place, or give a soft, non-creepy compliment about the clothes the person's wearing. Ask a question. If you're brave, offer them a drink. You might still get rejected, but your chance of 'success' will increase dramatically while your feeling of embarrassment decreases in equal measure. On a cold call, you're starting a relationship. Think about the person you're talking to, what would help them. Ask questions. Give them something valuable. Don't sell.

We've not done a great deal of cold calling to grow Genie Goals, except at the very beginning, the first two or three months. We soon realised that it wasn't going to pay off for us then. We wanted to create a strong agency brand and led this with what we thought was going to be an irresistible proposition for any brand: our proprietary tech and our performance model proposition, which at the time was very unique. The proposition had appeared in PPC but it wasn't unprecedented; search affiliates had been doing it for ten years, delivered in a different way, and in the agency environment one other agency was already offering it. We were like Apple with smartphones: we saw that the approach existed but was marginal, uncelebrated and unfashionable at best. We made it a thing – a thing that delivered results and made a statement.

The way the performance model worked is that we'd agree a fixed cost of sale (COS) with our customers and that was all they'd pay us – a commission out of which we'd pay the media spend, the money we invested in marketing to drive these transactions. So say we would drive £100K in sales from Google Ads, and we'd agreed a 20 percent COS; the customer would pay us £20K. If to drive that £100K we spent less than the agreed 20 percent, then we'd make a profit. The better we did, the more profit we'd make. But if we drove £100K in sales and spent more than £20K doing it, then we'd make a loss and our customer would lose nothing.

We thought that every retail brand on the planet would be super attracted by a proposition so strong, one that illustrated such confidence in our own abilities and tech. The tech was the backbone of our proposition. Before Genie Goals existed, its sister company Genie Ventures was already running a cluster of comparison websites and investing heavily in PPC. None of the bidding technologies available were good enough to drive large volumes at the low margins they faced. So Paul, Genie Ventures' co-founder and CTO, probably the smartest man I've met in my entire life, built a piece of technology that was designed to manage AdWords bids in the most granular way possible. The objective was to assign each keyword the best bid across products, geographical areas, time of the day, day of the week, lead time and more. So basically, the user could pay for a keyword what it was really worth based on its conversions. The results were outstanding: virtually overnight, COS halved and revenue spiked.

They tried this with one retail brand, 'friend of Genie', only to see the same results. The decision to take Genie Goals to market as an agency proposition came easily. The idea remained an idea for a while as Paul and Ciaron, MD at Genie Ventures, had their hands full with the publishing side of the business, the comparison search engines. When Ciaron and I talked about me coming in to run Genie Goals, I was pumped to grow the agency because of the strong proposition. But it was just me, and selling wasn't the only thing on my plate. We had to prove the model before we could form a business development team, and before I could invest in marketing, so cold calling seemed to make sense. I could do 40, 50 calls a day and reach loads of people to tell them about the amazing proposition, the tech and the performance model.

It didn't work. We realised that people didn't understand the COS model, it was too out-of-the-box at the time. It confused the living light out of people. Especially on the phone. So, after the first couple of months of cold calling, I chose to invest the time I had on events instead. We were targeting large retail brands and cold calling proved ineffective for us – it would take a few calls to get to speak to the right person, which resulted in a follow-up email with "more info", as requested. Most attempts to deliver the "more info" in a face-to-face meeting instead of on the phone were rejected on the basis that more people had to see the info, and before investing time in a meeting, they wanted to see something.

Fair enough. The way we go about pitching is based on a high level of confidence that we can make a big difference to performance. If we don't feel we can, then we'd rather not take the client on. This was especially true back then, when we only offered a performance model. We still apply the same rule today – if we can't bring massive value, we don't take the client on. It takes a considerable number of weeks before we are familiar with the client's tone of voice, USPs, ways of working and user behaviour on their site. If a customer joins Genie Goals to then leave after, say, six to nine months, we'd not make much profit, if any at all.

The first phase is always front-loaded in terms of workload. So we carry out a full account audit that allows us to tell the potential customer exactly what we'd change on the account and why, what we'd change it to and what kind of performance uplift they could expect as result. Therefore, before we pitch, before we can send the "more info", we need to carry out an audit, which takes time and means we need to access the prospects' accounts.

Time isn't an issue – you must invest the time to win

customers if you are offering something special, non-standard and remarkable. The problem was gaining access to their data. Through cold calling, the level of trust on which we can leverage is tiny, below ground. Most large brands are hesitant to give you access to important data, such as data in Adwords and Analytics, without strong trust. Remember, back then we were nobody. We had one small client and that was it. No awards, no top ranking in EMEA, no cool global brands on our website, no case studies. We had zero reputation. This was one of the issues we faced with cold calling.

If we'd had a business development executive, we might have got them to do 60 calls a day with the objective of bringing home one audit per week. That would have been very satisfactory, and if we knew then what we know now, we might have done it. But we didn't. We thought our performance-only model and our cutting-edge tech would blow the commerce manager's sock's off. But we couldn't get in front of them with the full message.

So we opted to speak at all the conferences we could. That would put us in a room with anywhere between 100 and 350 people right in our target market, who were taking the time to come and learn about what was happening in the digital marketing industry that might benefit the brands they were working for. These were, in theory, motivated prospects, happy to listen. We did that and it worked. My strong Italian accent and my very outspoken, high-energy style were very unusual in the digital marketing industry, and I captured the attention of the audience. Then, once they started a conversation with us, the Cambridge PhD-built tech and the talented team (two people working on the publisher side of the business) got them sold.

In some ways, we have been spoilt by our uniqueness. A good

209

dose of luck helped us grow without having to rely on cold calling. But that was us. We were a very particular business with a very specific offering. Not necessarily better, just very specific, with a very specific set up at a very specific time, when it was unusual for agencies to have their own tech (it is less so now), and very unusual – unheard of, really – for agencies to offer a performance model. Again, this is more normal, and therefore better understood, today. Plus, we offer other more traditional models today too, as do you, I suspect.

At the time of writing, we are onboarding a Senior Business Development Manager to our team and I expect cold calling will come into the strategy. My feeling with cold calling for us today is that we should cold call with the softest call to action possible – get people at one of our free events, or arrange an interview (for our Digital Marketing Show), because we like their story and anything that adds value to them with zero requests from us. An audit would probably naturally follow, especially now that, thanks to our reputation and track record, we enjoy almost instant credibility.

But if you target smaller businesses, if you are a digital agency and can and want to work with restaurants, dentists, shops, accountants, lawyers, etc., then cold calling can be very effective. When I was running a much smaller marketing consultancy agency and a graphic design agency, cold calling is how we won the vast majority of our business. We were able to reach decision makers in one or two calls. There was often no audit to do because they were new to the platforms, or the audits were small and could be done quickly.

If you select your prospects well, you should be able to drive loads of incremental business easily, because, with new or smaller advertisers, they opportunities for 'quick wins' should be plenty and the barrier to entry, the trust required, should be low, as the data they'd be sharing wouldn't be as important to them as it might be to larger players. With customers like these, you can add value and make money in the process relatively easily. You should be able to find clients for whom you can add considerable uplift with minimal work. Cold calling can work well to start a conversation with these people.

The way I'd approach it is still the same way I used to grow our small consultancy agency: build a structure, decide on the level of activity required and stick to that. I needed to make 60 calls per week. This would drive five appointments, which would get me one client. It was reliable. It was a numbers game, and it still is. Give yourself a 'data-period' – a period of time during which the main objective of the cold calling campaign is to understand how many calls you need to make to secure a client. That gives you data. Once you do that, you'll realise that the numbers are pretty reliable, the same way that site CR is – it can fluctuate but it doesn't tend to swing wildly for no reason.

At that point, you can influence the CR of your calls by tweaking the script, the target audience, the time of the calls, etc. It can be a fun exercise. You will get to a point at which you'll know that for every X calls, Y won't be reachable, Z will say no, XX will say maybe (don't call these back, have them call you) and YY will say yes to a meeting. You will also learn that for every so many meetings, you'll win a gig. Once you get to that, all you need to do is to focus on hitting the numbers. You can almost forget about each call and simply focus on the activity: if you call that many people, if you follow the script, you will get new business. It's an incredible feeling, as close to certainty as you'll ever get in most sales jobs. If cold calling is for you, the following tips can be very helpful and save you tonnes of time and money.

211

Have a list

Spend some time researching and populating a spreadsheet or CRM with all the contacts that you want to reach out to, and do this in bulk. Dedicate periodic sessions exclusively to do this, ensuring each session is at least two hours long, preferably longer. The reason is that it'll take you a little while to get into the rhythm and get into flow. The number of contacts you will find and insert in your list in the first hour or so is likely to be less than half of the number of contacts you'll be able to add in each subsequent hour. Once you have sacrificed the first hour to warming up and getting into flow, make the rest of the time count by sticking with it as long as you either can afford to or are able to keep your productivity up – there will be a point after a while at which your productivity will begin to decline because of fatigue or lack of flow, and you'll plateau.

When I was growing my first marketing consultancy agency in the UK, I used to spend Mondays building the list for the week. I wanted to average 150 calls per week. It's important to note that by 'calls' I mean dials, which includes those who don't answer, those I can't reach, etc. This can seem time consuming and boring. It is both. That's why, as soon as you have a list that closely represents your target market, the best gift you can give yourself is to outsource this to a freelancer or delegate it internally to a junior (interns are great for this as it provides value to you and teaches them business in the real world, with their hands in the grease).

Just as you need to get into flow when researching, you also need to get into flow when calling. The more you call, the better you'll get. The first few calls will be more difficult – you'll be more likely to feel nervous, and more likely to talk nonsense and come across like a nervous teenager asking someone out for the first time. As you do more calls, the nerves will ease and you'll begin to enjoy it more, sounding more and more smooth and confident – I'm talking Joey-from-Friends confident.

Short and simple

Prospect: Hello?
Caller: Hello, I'm John from COMPANY, how are you today?
Prospect: Good thank you. How can I help you?
Caller: I'm calling from COMPANY and I wanted to talk to you about how you can achieve 1, 2, and 3 using our product, which does X, Y and Z. We have a gazillion case studies and reach all of the people in the world. The way it works is that we take your brand and do A, B and C and then your customers… blah blah blah blah.

This kind of intro raises the strongest of guards. Instead, keep it short and simple, and ask questions. Read the section on weak language, later in the book. It'll help you get this perfect. Here's a better version of that call.

Prospect: Hello?
Caller: Hello, my name is Luca. I appreciate we don't know each other, and I've just cold called you, so I'll be short and to-the-point. Are you guys at BRAND/COMPANY 100 percent happy with the performance of your FILL IN THE BLANK channel today?

Prospect potential response 1: "Yes we are actually." At this point they might go on to tell you more about why they are happy, and you need to shut up and listen until the person at the other end of the phone is totally finished. This is so important that I am tempted to repeat that sentence 20 times. Shut up, be quiet and listen. Here is where the important information is delivered – you might hear stuff that you can either use now or in the future when you get back in touch. Also, by listening, you build rapport: everybody likes to talk about themselves and likes to be listened to.

Prospect potential response 2: "We are reasonably happy; of course you can always be happier, right?" And again, here they might elaborate and start talking more. If not, I'd encourage you to make them do so by saying things like: "Tell me more, what would make you happier with the performance of your FILL IN THE BLANK channel?"

Prospect potential response 3: "Actually, no, we have some challenges and..." they'd tell you more. Bingo.

There are clearly other possible responses, but these three cover most of what I've encountered in my many years of cold calling. Here's how you could reply to each of these responses. As always, they are here to provide guidance, inspiration and the principles. These are not scripts.

Your reply to response 1: "That's great to hear. I believe that if every agency did a great job for their customers, there would be more business for every other agency too because the advertisers' confidence in agencies would increase and bring more work. If in the future you ever want a fresh pair of eyes, I'd be happy to have one of our XX specialists complete an account audit for you, free of charge. That would tell you exactly what we don't feel is optimal in the account and why, what we think it should be changed to and what results such changes are likely to bring in terms of performance. That way you'd be able to make informed decisions going forward and optimise the account even more. Is it okay if I reach out in three months to offer the free audit?" At this stage, they might actually even ask for the audit now. It's happened to us before. If not, then you have just made a great contact – treat them well, add value and they might convert in time.

Your reply to response 2: As in V1, offer the audit, but this time you have the licence to offer it now. If they don't jump on it, you can always go back to the softer three-month sell.

Your reply to response 3: You don't need me to tell you what to do here right? I will anyhow: shut up and listen. Get the audit arranged and start the sale cycle. If they are not happy and have an agency, you might have to help them gain trust in you. I cannot tell you how you do this, it depends on who you are and who you're talking to. Case studies, references and achievements such as awards can help.

To prepare for cold calling, go back to the previous chapters and use THE WHY and THE WHAT. These will help you with your responses and the whole conversation will be much smoother.

Ask questions and listen, listen, listen.

I've mentioned this already, but it's worth repeating. The importance of asking questions and listening to the answers is always underestimated. Asking questions is great for building rapport, and for finding things out that might help you offer the best solution, now or in the future. It's also important because it helps you gather data and spot patterns in the industry, which you can use to inform future decisions. The fact that selling is about giving people what they need is an illusion. **Selling is about giving people what they want. The difference is enormous. Think and you will realise what they need. Listen and you will know what they want.**

We like people who listen more than we do those who talk. When you cold call people, being liked is your number one priority. It reminds me of a day when I was 22, selling the ugly version of the *Yellow Pages* to organisations all over Italy. I managed to secure an appointment with a CMO of a large organisation through his secretary. I pitched up for the meeting and as soon as I took out the big YP-type book to show my prospective client the 'opportunity', he stopped me in my tracks and told me that he knew the product I was about to offer very well. He told me the whole story of the company, the story of the industry, stuff that even I didn't know, and I was supposed to be the expert. He said he wasn't interested and listed exactly why. It made sense so I accepted it and put the book away.

I then asked how he knew so much about the advertising industry and the company I was representing. He told me the whole story and more. From there, one question led to another and another still. We soon found ourselves talking about completely different topics and I learnt all about his experience, background, likes and even family members. He talked for 30 or 40 minutes; I talked for five or six. I then said something along the lines of: "It's really great talking with you, you are a very interesting man and this was the most enjoyable 'no' I have ever received in sales." Half jokingly I then went on to say: "But now I'd better go to my next appointment so that I can get the 'yes' I need to hit my target." He said nothing for 20 or 30 seconds and then he said: "How much did you say that vertical space was?" Confused, I replied: "990." He said: "Do it for 900 and I'll sign it!" "Why?" I asked. "Because that amount of money is nothing for our organisation and I want to help you. You are a bright guy and I have a feeling that building a relationship might be beneficial in the future, when you sell a product I can use." That was such a big lesson for me.

I'm not suggesting that you'll pitch up to people who don't want to buy and sell to them just by listening. But the line is often less defined than this. When it comes to choosing between two agencies with very similar propositions and offerings, customers will choose the one that they like more, and people like people who listen. So listen, for goodness' sake. It really frustrates me when people try to sell to me and don't listen; I want them to win, I want them to sell to me, but then I lose trust in the product they're offering because I don't have the confidence that they know what I want. Because they haven't bloody listened. Listen. #listen. @listen.

To close the cold calling section, I thought I'd include a short list of things you can say that generally never work and a list of things that often do. More on communication later in the book.

What to say and not to say

Not to say:

- **"The reason for my call"**: You're about to tell them the reason. Just do that.

- **"I am calling on behalf of"**: You are calling as you. The company name will come later.

- **"I am calling from a company called"**: It makes the company sound like a third party. "I'm John, from Agency X" is better.

- **"Did I catch you at a bad time?"**: The answer will virtually always be yes.

- **"Can I speak to the person who deals with X?"**: Sale sale sale. Find out who the right person is. You have LinkedIn, remember? Can't find it? Call another company.

To say:

- **"We have done work with SIMILAR CUSTOMER and..."**: Similar customer is likely to be a competitor. That's likely to interest them.

- **"I know you are busy and I won't waste your time"**: Shows respect and empathy.

- **"If we were to be able to do this for you, would you be interested in collaborating?"**: Direct and sensible question. Shows a no-nonsense approach and confidence.

- **"I have called because, having done similar things successfully with BRAND X, I am hoping we can do it for you. If you are happy to meet with me, I will invest the time to do the work, the research and give you concrete illustrations of what return you could see. All I ask is that you meet with me once this is ready so we can have a meaningful and constructive conversation. If we win your business, great. If we don't, we will bring value with the research, which you get to keep and we learn how to improve. Deal?"**

Like I said at the beginning of this chapter, cold calling isn't for every organisation, but I hope the information here has opened your mind to it in a different way. Hopefully I was able to show you that you can successfully use cold calling to start conversations and, if you do this right, these are likely to pay off in the long run.

Actions

- Set aside one day for list creation and one for reporting. Mondays and Fridays are good for these.

- Write your script, not to stick to, but rather to give you guidance, especially when you first get into cold calling.

- Practice, even during normal day-to-day conversations, the art of asking questions and then being quiet. Listen.

- Make sure you know what to say and what not to say. Reread the last section if you need to.

THE PITCH

When that's all said and done, you'll have to pitch to prospective clients. All your work done in marketing and selling led you here. The pitch is where the sale is closed. You have built an incredible business, a remarkable team, a fantastic training program and kick-ass sales and marketing strategy for your business. Now you have to pitch. There are many books that address selling and pitching; in this section, I've included the 20 to 30 percent of strategies that are likely to give you 70 or 80 percent of the results. This is the stuff that has worked for us at Genie, and the stuff that other agencies have done to bring in business and success through pitching.

So where do you start? You start by understanding as much as you can when you first come into contact with a prospective customer. Whether they reached out to you or you reached out to them, you want to understand all the important aspects of their business and objectives before you even start creating the pitch. Here we'll go into some of the aspects that are relevant to us and probably you – take what's relevant and replace what isn't, come up with stuff based on your historical data or an educated guess. What I'm describing here, just like throughout the book, are the principles rather than the specifics.

Budget

You have to understand the size of the budget. If you are a marketing agency and you deal with paid media, then you want to understand the size of the budget that the prospective customer has to invest in paid media. If you are a development agency, a graphic design agency or any other project-based agency, you want to understand the size of the budget for the given project, because this will frame the conversation. Understanding the budget will immediately let you know what resources you can dedicate to the account, the type of help that you might need, and in general, the type of workload and shape the project is likely to bring.

I remember 10 or so years back, I started a graphic design agency, only because many of my marketing consulting customers were asking for the service. I hired a friend who was a graphic designer and started offering the service. One day we received a call from one of the most prestigious law firms in London – they wanted a total redesign. I was so excited I think I actually clapped during the phone call. I spent three weeks preparing a pitch and travelled to London, only to hear that their budget was £3K. They wanted a logo, more than 40 attorney page profiles, headed paper, a website with a complex structure, and business cards. £3K. Are you serious? £3K. In the end, we were extremely lucky and slowly managed to persuade them that we needed more like £30K. We got the contract, and today, more than 10 years after I sold the agency to my former business partner, they are still a customer. We were lucky, but I can tell you plenty of stories without the happy ending.

Find out what the budget is, then you can act accordingly, prepare and have your facts and deck ready to back your argument. If the budget is larger than you think it should be, you can make the strategic decision to inform them and look very honest or offer the absolute best possible solutions with all the bells and whistles you can find.

Timeline

The second thing that you want to understand is the timeline. Are they looking for an agency now because they are desperate? Are they looking to change the current agency because they've just had enough? Is this urgent or are they researching for next year or next quarter? Is it perhaps the case that a new manager came in and wants to make an impression, do her job well and so decided to investigate what other agencies might have to offer?

It's very important, critical in fact, that you understand the timeline; this will shape the dynamic of your immediate day-to-day business and the decisions you'll make in the near future. Often people forget to do that, and they almost reach the pitching process before they realise that the project is more urgent that they thought and they don't have the resources to deliver it. Or the opposite may happen – they realise that the project is not likely to start for six or even nine months. This happens a lot. Don't let it happen to you, ask the question.

Today I received an RFP (request for proposal) from an e-commerce manager who used to work at one of our customers and then moved on to another global brand. Lilly (let's call her) wants us to pitch for the performance marketing channels: PPC, shopping, paid social, retargeting, etc. It's a great opportunity. She actually made contact the first time regarding this about a month ago. I have very gently chased a couple of times, and today she sent the RFP. I got really excited – the account is massive and the budgets are large. We looked at the timeline. They are not looking to make a decision till April next year. It's now the beginning of September. They've got September, October and November to research, December for the pitching and January for the decision. The new agency will start in April.

Do you realise that we're talking about seven months here? Without knowing this, I might have gotten all excited and perhaps moved things around so that we could prepare the pitch – this is an important brand – only to realise that they're not going to make a decision until January. "Luca, shut up! This is common sense" I hear you say. Well, then common sense isn't that common these days. This stuff happens every single day: agencies get halfway through the pitching process and never ask the questions: "when are you looking to make a decision? And where are you looking to start?" Know the freaking timeline.

The WHY

Point number three is the WHY. You must absolutely understand their WHY, their pain points. Why are they looking for an agency? Are they replacing a current agency? If so, why are they replacing their current agency? What is it that they're not happy with in the current service they receive? You need to understand the pain points because if what makes them unhappy now with their current agency is something you cannot provide the solution to, then you are much better off addressing that at the very beginning. You don't want to onboard the client to then disappoint them later. Even if you are desperate for new business right now, this is not a good idea – it will cost everybody money and time. It costs because the onboarding is time consuming and my suspicion is that if you bring in a client and they only stay two or three months, you'll probably lose money because the work is often front-loaded. It costs them because getting agencies to pitch is expensive in terms of resources.

The other thing that can happen is that you burn the client.

The client will lose confidence, not only in you but in the entire industry. So be careful when you onboard clients from other agencies, make sure that you understand what the pain points are and ensure that you can satisfy those. We'll cover more on this shortly when we talk about auditing.

Another scenario: let's say they are looking to bring in an agency because they want to move from in-house to outsourcing. Then the question is: what are the pain points of doing it in-house? And again, you must make sure that the agency solution that you offer is able to overcome those pain points. Is the organisation perhaps very new? If this is the case then you need to be mindful of it from the beginning, because when you work with new advertisers and new organisations, there are many factors that influence how you manage such accounts. There's a much larger portion of time that goes into educating them, holding their hands in making some of their important decisions, and generally helping them understand the landscape, as it can be really overwhelming for new organisations that haven't been through it. If you are used to working with more experienced teams, then you might overlook some of the important reassurance pieces and might lack empathy. Lack of empathy can destroy a relationship. So make sure that you understand the circumstances and their WHY.

Questions like these can open up very insightful and useful conversations:

- "What are the top two things you like about the current agency?"

- "What are the top two things you are frustrated by in the current agency or in-house solution?"

- "What are you looking to achieve personally in your role?"

- "What can an agency do that would make your job here a lot more enjoyable?"

But once you've asked, get out of your own way, be quiet and listen.

The audit

Once you've understood their WHYs, their pain points, the next step is to go into an audit. Now, if you run a paid advertising operation, PPC, paid social, or anything of that kind, you are able to carry out an audit on the current activities. You'll probably be asked to sign a non-disclosure agreement (NDA) and get the access to their account to do an audit. At Genie Goals, we invest an incredible amount of time in doing a very comprehensive and accurate audit before we even prepare a pitch for a prospective customer. Once we've done the audit, we'll tell the prospective client exactly:

- What we don't like in the account and why.

- What the performance implications such imperfections might cause.

- What we would change those things to, and how.

- What positive impact such changes are likely to have on performance.

This way, we manage expectations and we can understand whether we can actually add value. **The number one secret in winning and retaining customers is adding real value.** If you cannot add real value, don't take the customer on. Simple. Only take customers on when you can add real value. And real value doesn't necessarily mean driving more performance. It could be better service, better understanding, better communication, better experience, or simply more synergy between the two parties. If you know what the client's WHYs and pain points are, then you'll be able to know whether you can add real value. The audit is a big part of determining exactly that.

Presenting the audit

We used to make the mistake of sending the audit and then sending the proposal next to it, as a separate document. I realised very quickly that people were reading the audit very carefully and attentively, but barely even looking at the proposal. It was apparent during the meeting that they knew the audit inside out, word for word nearly, but almost looked as if they had never seen any of the slides in the proposal.

So I had the rather brilliant idea (brag) to embed the audit into the proposal. The way this looks is that as a prospective customer, you would see one slide, for example, on "Best practice and account structure". Then the second slide would be titled "Currently in Your Account" which would describe the current structure. The next slide would be "What We Would Do" – this would tell the customer what we'd propose to do on the account for that particular section. Then the next slide would be, for example, "Keyword targeting", illustrating our ways of doing it, the best practice. This would be followed by a slide on "Currently in your account" and again, one about "What We Would Do", and so on. I basically alternate slides as follows:

- Our methodology.

- The findings from the audit.

- What we would do in that account.

- The likely results of the changes we'd make, where applicable.

The results? Ridiculously good. Doing this keeps people glued to the screen, engaged and interested. They read every single slide or page in the proposal. And this was probably the most ingenious thing that I ever came up with when it comes to selling (more bragging).

THE KIS vs THE KIL

A couple more words on the pitching document, the deck. Remember the story about when we went to pitch to what would have been our largest customer and screwed up because we took it for granted that we were going to adopt all useful targeting options in the Google Ads interface? We learned from that experience, and the day after that pitch, our skeleton deck went from 15 slides to 94 slides. From that moment on, I promised myself I would never lose a pitch again because I'd left anything out.

We started detailing in the deck every single thing that we thought was relevant for the client. We realised that we had developed what I call 'advanced practitioners' blindness'. We didn't see what the customers saw. When writing emails, social media posts, reports and even in verbal communication, I am a massive fan of 'less is more', of keeping it short and simple. But I am never going to make that mistake again in a pitch, and so, whilst we use the fewest words possible to make each point, in the spirit of keeping it short and simple, the deck itself is massive and always will be. In building decks, KIS (keep it simple or keep it short) loses in this case. KIL wins. KIL is 'keep it long'. You can always skip slides, you can always go fast, you can always ignore slides. But the moment at which you don't have a detail in there and the customer questions it, there's no saving yourself because you're saying: "Oh, we take that for granted." That just sounds like an excuse. So this is my advice to you: KIL, keep it long and skip slides if you have to.

Ask for the close or next steps

You went for a pitch and you've done a great job. Bravo. Now the most important thing to do in the pitch is to ask very directly: "Are you satisfied with the information we provided? Is there anything more we need to tell you? Was there anything else you wanted us to tell you that we didn't?" If you can, (and in the agency environment, especially if working with larger clients, often you can't), close the sale then and there. "Good, are you happy to go ahead? We can start in the next week or two."

Again, often that won't be possible, in which case you still want to be asking when decisions will be made – asking things like: "When are you guys looking to make a decision?" is perfectly fine and no one will get offended because you asked. People don't mind telling you if they know. Sometimes they won't know because they don't yet have an agreed date. In those cases, they could just give you the ballpark, whether it's a couple of weeks, a month or longer. That allows you to know when to follow up with an email or with a call. It might seem like I'm stating the obvious, but when I asked the agencies I interviewed for this book whether they knew when their prospective customers were going to make a decision, the responses were skewed heavily towards "no".

Pitching is very, very, very important, even if you don't win the business. *Even if you don't win the business.* **Pitching is**

very important, even if you don't win the business. It's so important, it deserves to be repeated. A "no" is just a "no today" if you are impressive during the pitch. If you are not, then it might be a "no forever", or a "hell no". The one thing that you can never afford to lose a pitch for is being unimpressive.

Put the time in – invest time in researching exactly what their WHYs are, what their pain points are, what their objectives are. Where do they want to go by working with you? What's their North Star? Find out more about the business, their story, their mission and talk about that. Learn all you can about them and you feed that back, talk about how your company's missions are aligned (if they are), how you like their story (if you do), feed the pain-points back, feed the solutions from the audit or analysis back, and make sure they know you understand them, not only as a prospective customer, not only as more cash in your bank, but that you truly understand their business and want to understand more. If you do all that, you are off to a bloody good start, I freaking promise you – you're ahead of 99 percent of the other businesses pitching for the gig. You might lose because of price, timeline, or many other reasons, but you must ensure that you never, ever lose because of quality. You must not lose because you were unimpressive. Research, research, research.

The meeting

You get there, in person – no more cushioned safety of emails and calls, you are there in the flesh. For you this might be heaven; this is where you thrive, this is where you like it. Or it might be hell. Here a few things that will help you like it even more if it's your heaven and like it enough to win some business if it's your hell.

Be you:

First and foremost, make sure that you are you. High-energy, introverted, inspirational, analytical, funny, not funny, just you, whatever you are. Be you. Show the customers that you've done the research. Talk about them all the time. Relate everything you describe to them. If you describe a process that you that you have internally, a methodology, a technology, make it relatable to them. Always include the context of what it would do for them. "Our team would do a great job with you because their specialism in retail allows your brand, BRAND NAME to do X, Y, and Z. You told me about that challenge you were wrestling with, this is exactly what our team is strong at. Our technology is built for situations like this, the autobidder works well for your brand because, since you have XX products in your catalogue, it can do A, B and C."

Always make it relatable to them but be you. Do this with your energy, with your character and with your personality; don't fake it, don't act the way you think they'd want you to act. They would know. The worst thing that you can do to yourself is to pretend and succeed with it because then you'd be stuck, you'd need to pretend for the rest of your life. Be you, no one in the world is better at being you than you.

Interact:

Make the meeting interactive. Ask questions during the presentation. Don't fall into the trap of presenting for 40 minutes and not asking for questions. Every now and again, ask things like: "Does that make sense to you? Have you been in this position before? How does that sound?" This gets the people in the room engaged and it gives you a sense of whether people are actually following and agreeing with what you are sharing. Remember the large contract we didn't win that we talked about earlier, in the 'More on 'No's' section? Had I done this with them, we might have won that gig.

Different energies:

It's always good to have two different people in the pitch if you can, with different personalities and areas of expertise: One strategy expert, for example, and a second person with a different type of energy who's a technical specialist. When choosing a partner to start a new business with, many make the mistake of choosing someone just like them. The right thing to do is choose someone who complements us, someone with skills opposite to ours.

It's the same in pitches. If you have opposite specialisms and personalities in the meeting, you have more chances to build rapport with the prospective customer without having to force a change in you, without having to pretend. If you see there is a bit of resistance or a lack of rapport, then your colleague can do more of the talking. If you find that you have an alpha male and somebody more relaxed, and the alpha male is not really going down well, use the other person. Let the other person lead the conversation.

The opposite is also true. I have a very strong personality – some love it, some hate it. Tom, the Head of Agency, and Imogen, Head of Account Excellence, are both very technical and a lot softer in their energy levels. Often I do the aspirational bit, I get customers excited about working with us because of the level of energy I bring, which is reflective of how we'd work in terms of pace and flexibility. But then I let Tom or Imogen do a lot of the talking on the technical stuff. Some customers just need me, they need my energy and push and so I do 90 percent of the talking. Others are the opposite, and I just need to be quiet because that specific customer works a lot better with the softer approach and energy Tom and Imogen bring.

The signs you want to pay attention to can include:

- They consistently and continuously engage in eye contact more with your colleague and when you are talking they look around.

- Their body faces your colleague a lot more than it does yours, even when you are talking.

- They nod a lot when your colleague speaks and not at all when you do.

- They ask your colleague questions and not you.

- They lean in when your colleague speaks and lean back when you do.

- They visibly approve and get excited about what your colleague says and not by what you say.

These are just a few of the signals that are important to read. Don't overdo it though. I normally look for clusters: two or three signals during the same meeting. Although this doesn't happen every day, it does happen sometimes, and it's important that you recognise it. It might just be a lack of rapport, which you can work on.

Once you learn to pay attention it's really quite obvious. In some cases, I can see that if I continue talking I might just screw the whole thing up, at which point I pass on the torch to my colleagues.

Be a true extension of their team:

Please forget that you work for you. Forget that you work for your agency. Forget you, altogether. When you pitch to a new customer and when you work with a recently acquired customer, I think it's important that you forget everything about you and just immerse yourself as much as you can in the customer.

You need to understand everything there is to understand about the client: their brand, their story, why they exist, what's important to them, what their values are, why are they doing what they're doing. Understand the WHYs, understand their services, their products, their dilemmas, their challenges, even the challenges that go beyond what you are trying to solve by selling the service or product that you sell.

It's one of the most important things you can do. It's not about you, it's about them. We always talk about this customer-centric era, this customer-centric strategy, this customer-centric protocol and procedure. But rarely do service businesses put their money where their mouth is. And as soon as they get to pitch to a customer, or certainly, as soon as they win the contract, it becomes all about the agency. "This is how <u>we</u> work". "This is what <u>we</u> can do". "This is how <u>we</u> are going to take this forward". And I believe 100 percent that's the wrong thing to do.

Work to understand the brand, their tone of voice, why they are where they are. And once you get to understand all of these points, you truly become an extension of the customer's team. If you become an extension of their team, it's no longer 'them' and 'you', it's no longer 'customer' and 'agency', it's no longer 'buyer' and 'service supplier'. It's <u>a team</u>. We are part of the same thing. **It becomes we.**

Send your staff to see the manufacturing plant if they've got one. Send your staff to talk to everybody in the company – customer services first, then merchandising, the packing and picking people, buyers, finance. Everyone you have access to. Try to understand their business inside out, and that will put you in a much better place to solve their issues, which become your issues.

During a pitch, I always say (and I always mean it): "This isn't you and us". I say to my client, "Let's not talk about the agency and the customer because that won't work. You'd end up spending loads of cash that goes to strangers who are supposed to manage one of the most important marketing channels for your business. It won't work. Let's instead talk about us. When things go wrong, and I can tell you that they will, because we'll push the boundaries, and because nobody's perfect, we will be scratching our heads together, asking ourselves what we must do. We will be there, not trying to hide what's gone wrong but trying to find a solution together. When things go well, then we'll celebrate together. It will become a collaborative exercise – an exercise for us to prove to you how good we are. Only then can we do a good job, not *for* you but *with* you. So if you're able and happy to open up to us and treat us like a newly acquired extension of your team, a new section of your company, then this has got every chance of going very far and creating a whole new level of success for this channel."

And I say this not because it's romantic, I say this not because it sells, I say this because it's true. The last thing you want to be doing is saying stuff like this if you don't mean it, or if you're not able to follow through and actually do what you say you're going to do.

But if this is the culture that you want to inject in your company, and you should absolutely want to do that, then say these things. And if you mean what you say, then the customer, or I should say your partners, will realise that you really mean it.

In the next few chapters, I've included some ideas about techniques and strategies for marketing your agency and winning business. Don't just CTRL-C and CTRL-V this. Use what fits in well with your business, with your agency, with your style and proposition and adapt or drop what doesn't. Use the next few chapters as inspiration for your very own strategies, techniques and winning formula.

Actions

- Write down a list of the things you need to find out before pitching. Budgets, timelines, reasons for the RFP and so on. The more you know, the more you can give them during the pitch.

- Prepare a good deck template. Then add the customer-specific parts as you gather information.

- Decide beforehand what you'd like to achieve in the meeting. If you're unsure of what's possible, you can ask the prospective customer so that you know what the steps after the meeting will be.

- Plan so that you can have a similar number of people in the meeting for balance, and bring people with different energies.

THE RELATIONSHIPS

We've looked at many ways to market and sell agency services, and by now I'm sure I've made it clear that I am a big believer in the fact that we must go after people, not brands. It's very easy to fall into the trap of winning business, and then putting that relationship into a 'machine', into a process whereby your account managers take over, and work the account doing everything they are supposed to, everything that you are paid for, but disregard the relationship aspect. The account managers will do what they have to, including maintaining the relationship. But that's not what I am talking about here. What I'm talking about here is you, the lead of the agency.

Whether you are the head of growth, the director, the MD, the CEO, whatever title you've decided to put next to your name on your business cards, building relationships with your customers is very important. I have made this mistake myself many times before and paid the price for it. I've made corrections and seen massive benefits as a result. Whilst your account managers have a relationship connected to the specific account, you want to have a more general relationship with the key contacts. The reason is very simple: **you want to be connected to the people and not the brand**. You work on the brand but you're connected to the people in the brand. Why? Because when people leave brand A and go to brand B, they will take you with them.

I could tell you many stories about this, but there's one in particular about a customer of ours, a large global organisation based in Italy that offers web-to-print and digital printing services. When we started working with them, their team was led by Andrew (not his real name), the Global Marketing Director. Andrew didn't have much to do with the account, it was David and his team who did. They were our point of contact for the day-to-day running of the campaigns. Andrew would come in for short periods during strategy meetings but that was really it for the most part. I made the point of building a relationship with Andrew, we got along well and eventually became good friends.

After about two years of working with us, the printing company restructured the team and, having received a fantastic offer from what's probably the most important fitness and wellness equipment brand in the world, Andrew decided to leave the company to join the much larger fitness equipment giant. Guess what: he took us with him to manage their paid media accounts. The agency that had the account before we took over really wasn't doing a great job. We did an audit, as we always do, and knew the account had massive room for improvement and enhanced performance, so we absolutely deserved to be there – we were going to add value and make things a lot better. But to be frank, I really don't think that we would have had the chance to pitch for that account had it not been for the relationship I had with Andrew.

It goes without saying that if we hadn't impressed everybody else in the team, if we hadn't delivered, if we hadn't convinced people that we could add value, and crucially, if we hadn't done a good job at Andrew's previous organisation, we certainly wouldn't have had the opportunity to pitch. All of these aspects are massively important. You have to be good, and you have to do a good job, that's a given. But without our relationship with Andrew, we might never have had the chance to pitch. There are many stories like this I could tell you, all of which would have the same message: build relationships beyond the day-to-day running of the accounts. PS we still work with the printing company too; the ROI on relationships is always massive.

But who do you build relationships with within an organisation? The answer is very simple, though perhaps counter-intuitive. You want to build a relationship with everyone. Absolutely everyone. "Everyone in the organisation? Luca, are you out of your mind?" No, not everyone in the organisation. The brand I was talking about just now has 7,000 employees, so that would be impossible. Connect with everyone in the team, everyone you come into contact with. Naturally, some relationships will become stronger than others, some will last and some won't, and some will grow stronger than others. The point here is that if you are regularly in meetings with the Head of E-Commerce, the Head of Acquisition, the Digital Marketing Manager, and the interim Digital Marketing Assistant, you should build relationships with them. All of them.

You don't put in an equal amount of time and effort with everyone, because that's just impossible and it'd be unnatural. Instead, you give every relationship the same opportunity to grow and then you nurture the ones that naturally grow. You know, like you do in life. Imagine you win a new customer, you go back to the office after the win and add some people on LinkedIn. You add everyone who was at the meeting. Everyone, including John, the intern. Why would you choose to invite only some people? Because of their seniority? That's a bit shitty, I think. That's the wrong message to be sending. You start the relationship with everyone in the same way, and then you let each one develop organically, naturally.

Remember, junior people grow up. Junior people progress in

their careers. The CEO of ASOS, Nick Beighton, was once a junior. I know of someone who was in a junior position at a brand we were working with, and she moved on to be the lead at another brand. She called us to pitch. Don't make the mistake of going after the job title, don't go after the company. Go after the people. Treat everyone the same.

But what does it actually mean to build a relationship? You meet somebody for the first time, you pitch, you win the account. So you've met them twice, three times, you're not gonna invite them to a family barbecue. You build a relationship naturally. You ask questions. You listen. Ask questions. Listen. Ask questions. Listen. Especially at the beginning. That way you find out what makes this person tick, what's keeps them up at night, what gets them out of bed in the morning. You understand their pain points, the stuff that makes them excited. You understand their family circumstances – do they have kids? What do they like doing on weekends? Do they like football? Motorcycle racing?

And if you do that, if you ask questions and listen, what will happen, or what's extremely likely to happen, is that you will find out more about people. Let's say you found that a new contact you made is into golf, and you are at home on a Sunday afternoon and you notice the US Open is on. The next morning, there's nothing stopping you from dropping this person an email saying, "Happened to watch the US Open yesterday. Loved it. What did you think of it? Have a great week."

That's how you build relationships. That's what you'd do when you meet someone at a friend's barbeque and exchange contact details. Too many people treat business contacts differently from personal contacts. Why? When you get on with people it doesn't matter where you met. The only reason we tend to get on more with people we meet in social circumstances is that we talk more about personal circumstances. There's no rule that says you can't do that with business contacts; you can, and it works when you ask questions and listen.

Do we do it on purpose? Of course. Do we send that message on purpose? Of course. But do we mean it? Absolutely. You should not mistake that for being fake. It's being better. It's being more than. The fact that you start doing something you wouldn't have done before, doesn't mean that you're being fake, it just means that you're changing. What you shouldn't do is say stuff you don't mean. If you haven't watched the game, don't fucking send that email. It's as simple as that. But if you did watch the game, and if watching the game you thought of that contact, then absolutely send that email.

Lastly, do special acts, stuff most others don't do. What I mean by that is to send people you have a relationship with a small personalised, heartfelt gift on special occasions you know of: birthdays, joining a new company, getting out of hospital, winning an award. Send them a gift, a personalised USB, or a personalised coffee mug, whatever suits. A small thing – a small thing goes a long way. It's not the money it costs that adds value, **it's the thought behind it**.

At Genie, we have an incredible amount of talent. I'm serious, I feel extremely blessed to have such talented people around me every day. One of these people is a talented young man called Joe Glover. We hired Joe as a Junior Marketing Manager. Very keen, very smart, and from the offset, you could tell that he had the ability to be a very, very, very good Marketing Manager. Why? Because he is a very, very, very good human being. Joe is amazing at building relationships. If I sit down and think, I can come up with good, thoughtful actions like the ones I just described; Joe thinks of these things naturally. Personalised gifts, handwritten letters, branded socks, Black Friday recovery packs, new job cards, and so on. And he wouldn't do it in a way that comes across salesy. He naturally has the ability to come up with ideas that touch people's hearts, and that's an incredible gift.

Joe is one of the most well-known and loved people in Cambridge. He runs a marketing meetup and has more members in his group after one year than networking groups that have been going for five years can even dream of. How? He builds relationships. Joe is very gifted and he is very natural at it. But luckily for the rest of us, it's a skill that you can develop. I personally improved on that skill by working with Joe. I used to less personable than I am today, more focused on getting the job done. Today I'm doing better, and I got that from Mr Glover. So you can't hide behind the 'that's not me' card. It's a skill that does your business well; it does your whole life well too, as you'll meet new friends as well as new customers.

Another thing that you can do to nurture relationships is to invite your customers to speak at your events. We talked about running your own events earlier, and if you invite people to speak, they will feel very grateful and chuffed. They will feel like you are treating them as a model customer. They will probably develop a stronger sense of closeness with your agency. They will probably feel that you hold them in very high esteem. And stuff like that strengthens the bond.

Some of you might be thinking, "Come on Luca, of course that's obvious. I know all that stuff." I know you know, but you'd forgotten. We forget these things. I do it all the time, and I see that colleagues and peers, people in other agencies forget all the time too. Follow people, build relationships with people, your customers as well as your prospects. If you just follow the brand, every time your target person changes, you'll be left to re-introduce yourself. Follow people and when they go to a new brand, one that you haven't targeted before, you won't need an introduction. Follow people, not brands.

Actions

- Do what you can to always remember to do small things that build relationships. Perhaps you could use a Post-It you can always see, reminding you to do the small things we've just discussed.

THE FEES

To conclude THE GROWTH section of THE AGENCY, we must touch on the pricing strategy – the fees. There are two main points to make here, which we'll look at in depth:

1. Your pricing strategy can greatly impact your 'first contact to pitch' conversion rate as well as your 'pitch to deal' one. Don't rush into thinking this means cheap = better. It doesn't, and neither does the opposite.

2. Your pricing strategy can greatly impact your margins. Again, this doesn't mean that you should raise your prices.

If you are anything like me, you have two different fee levels: The one you'd like to charge and the one you actually charge.

They are different, and not acknowledging this is dangerous. When we first launched, we averaged £1.5K gross profit per client per month. A few years on, we were at £4.5K per client per month. At the time of writing, we are at £7K per client per month, and in 2023 we'll be at over £12K per client per month. This isn't because we are now charging more than we did a few years ago for the same service, or that we'll charge more in 2023 than we do now for the same service. It's because we add new services, new tech, new channels, and we manage larger budgets. Back in 2015, we only run PPC and shopping. Today, we run PPC, shopping, remarketing, affiliates, social, CSS and marketplaces, plus training and consultancy. Back in 2015, we managed budgets of up to £100K. Today, some of our clients spend more than £250K a month each on one channel alone. Our tech is more advanced and our credentials are radically different.

Your fee goal

It's vital that you have a fee goal in mind for the future, whilst at the same time, setting realistic fees for the present. Be careful not to undersell yourself, though. When brands see fees that are too low, red flags go off. "Are these guys any good?" "Can they afford to put in the time we need?" You might actually put some people off.

Do some research. Who are you competitors today? Not the ones that you aspire to be, the ones who are at a level of turnover, customers and size similar to you. What do they charge? Take the lowest-priced and the highest-priced and then decide where you sit. If you go towards the low end, why do you do that? What's the strategy? Is it because you can automate more? Is it so you can win more customers at the beginning and collect case studies to build a portfolio? Being priced at the low end isn't necessarily a bad thing if it's planned, if that's part of the strategy.

In the past, we have strategically gone into some relationships charging a lot less than we should have, but we made sure that the client knew we were doing it for a good reason. Typically, the reason was that the customer was a very well-known brand which could help us get credibility when we were still very small. At times, we still charge less than we should today, mainly when we find a new brand with high potential but low funds to start with. Many of these go on to grow and become full-paying customers that are extremely loyal to us.

If you decide to price yourself above what your competitors charge, why do you do that? Can you justify it? What is the added value you bring?

Fee increase

If you believe that you should charge more, do it. Don't be afraid of raising your fees; most of the time, your customers won't mind, and new customers will accept it more easily than you might fear. If you find customers who cannot afford you, that is the best reason to lose a pitch. We've had several potential customers who could not come with us because we were above their budget. They started somewhere else and some came with us later, once they grew.

Invest the increased profit

Depending on your business model, raising your prices even by just 10 percent can have a gigantic impact on your bottom line, mainly because that's where price increases go. It can make you a radically different business, way more profitable. The mistake that I know you're not going to make after having read this far into the book is cashing in that profit. That would be a very silly thing to do in your GROWTH phase. Instead, what you are going to do is invest it: invest it to hire new talent, invest it to provide a better service to your existing customers, which in turn positively impacts your retention, your referrals, or perhaps increases your profit per customer, if they end up buying more services from you as result of your investment in new or better services. You, better than anyone, know where to invest the extra profit.

Most of the time, there are opportunities to charge more without your customers raising any objections. Explore these opportunities. Don't do what you've always done just because it's always been done that way. I like to tell the story of 28-year-old Maria who's cooking a whole roast pig. She puts it on the tray, she chops the feet off and sticks the tray in the oven. A friend witnessing the scenes asks: "Maria, why did you chop the feet off? Just curious." Maria replies: "Not sure actually. Mum, why do we do it?" Mum says: "No idea actually. Grandma?" Grandma, who was giggling softly while all this was going down, looks at Maria and says: "I don't know why you do it. I did it because my tray was too small!"

Net profit

I couldn't have written this book without a word on net profit. We won't dwell on it too much, it's a big topic, and, depending on where you are on your journey, you might need specialist advice on this. But it's worth sharing a few important notions which will be very helpful to most agencies, especially if you don't feel particularly in control of your net margins.

Driving more revenue year-on-year is good, it's a sign of growth, but it means little when it comes to profitability. **Revenue is a vanity metric more often than not.**

Based on research conducted by The Wow Company[1], a firm of accountants specialised in working with digital agencies, most agencies in the UK end up doing free work for their customers. This is caused by ad hoc requests that are not priced or billed, size of projects increasing but not being reflected in the fees, and the lack of price increases failing to keep up with increases in overheads and running costs. The Wow Company's annual agency benchmark report, BenchPress, uncovered that 40 percent of agencies in the UK do project scoping for free, slicing their margins especially when there's no proper new customer enquiries filtering process in place. They also report that the UK average for billable time tracked by agencies is 63

---

1 https://www.thewowcompany.com/

percent of total waged time, but the goal should be 75 percent. In short, we're all under-billing.

At Genie, profitability is something that we purposely didn't pay full attention to for the first four or five years. We knew we were profitable, but we never stopped to measure it or plan for profit strategically. We wanted to be aggressive and grow, this was where our focus was. We invested ahead of the curve intentionally and that paid dividends.

As the company evolved and grew, whilst we still aimed to grow aggressively, we needed to be more in control of our margins as new elements might have affected our bottom line. There have been team restructures, new roles that are not necessarily directly contributing to profit, such as the Training & Development Manager, Head of Account Excellence and Head of Agency, which require a more structured approach to profitability in order to remain healthy. We started becoming a little more disciplined and, amongst other things, we started tracking the time staff spend on customers' accounts.

This is just step number one. You absolutely need to track the time that your employees spend on different projects and different clients. You don't people to feel that you are micromanaging and controlling what they do; it's really important that they understand that this is an exercise to safeguard their time and to make sure that projects don't get more time than assigned unless this is a conscious decision.

There are different tools that can help you track time on projects, and I've listed these in THE TOOLS section further on.

Next, you need to start planning, not so much how much *revenue* you want to drive (that's a vanity metric, remember?) but how much *profit* you want to drive.

If you set goals based on profit, then you'll be able to reverse-engineer that, so you know the number of clients you need and the revenue they have to generate to get to your net profit target. Part of getting to that point is to understand your hourly rate. This is typically broken down by seniority of the team members involved in each project.

In a recent webinar I attended with The Wow Company, they reported that the average hourly rate tiers of the top-performing agencies in the UK are:

- Director £130

- Senior £100

- Mid-Level £94

- Junior £85

Next is how you go about charging your clients. This is simple to do once you have your hourly rates nailed down. Your project lead gives you the estimated hours required per month for each seniority level, and that gives you your fee. The accuracy with which you or your team are able to forecast the hours required is obviously key here. Some agencies manage to agree 'dynamic' charging models that change in each phase of the project. It can be extremely hard to budget accurately for large projects, so some agencies quote for each phase – they estimate that phase one will cost X, and once they finish that phase, they have a better idea of what the next one will actually entail.

Another very important element of profitability is to make sure that it's in the culture. Often profitability is something that is discussed by the senior management team, at best and only at board level at worst. Instead, I believe that it's super important that profitability is understood and accepted by and in the awareness of every single member of staff.

Profit isn't why you're doing what you're doing. You are doing what you're doing because of your big WHY, your mission. Profit allows you do to that.

Profitability is the petrol that gets the car moving, we don't buy cars so that we can fill them up with petrol. We fill them up with petrol because we need them to take us places. Your agency doesn't do what it does for the profit, but it needs the profit to do what it needs to do.

It's important that your staff understand and accept that. I strongly recommend that you begin to introduce the concept of profitability and why it is important early on, normalise talking about profit. It is also important for your staff to know that charging for ad-hoc requests and increased workload is a way to assign the adequate resource to the project which in turn safeguards their time. Failing to charge more for extra work will make assigning additional resources hard and this might mean that whoever works on that project needs to work longer and harder to keep up. Achieving the target profitability on projects allows the company to be able to invest more and the staff to safeguard their time. The customer is also a winner, as their project will receive the attention it needs.

There's an incredible amount that can be said about profitability. I've just signed up to a five-day workshop by The Wow Company, which is designed to help us be even more savvy in this area. I suggest you do something similar and invest in first understanding where you're at, and then knowing what steps you need to take to achieve your profitability goals.

Actions

- Do some benchmarking so you know the market.

- Work on a narrative to make the fee discussion irrelevant.

251

How can you make the fees irrelevant by showing that the value you bring will greatly overshadow your fees?

- Decide on your fee goals. What do you want your fees to be (probably dictated by your revenue or profit goals) in the next year, two years and three years?

- Decide how you're going to bridge the gap between your fee today and your fee in the future. New services? Positioning? Decide this now – be ready to adapt and change but start with a plan now.

- Work on understanding your net margin goals.

- Track project times.

- Set profit goals and not revenue goals.

SECTION THREE: REPEAT

This is a relatively short but super important section of the book. It's called REPEAT, but it could be called SCALE all the same. It's about scalability and the ability to do what you've done twice, three times over. How do you go do the next level?

See it this way: Section one was about building the new house for you to let out. You dug and built solid foundations that can take the weight of what's to come. You put down the bricks, completed the interior and decorated, and it looks awesome. Section two was about putting tenants in the house – good tenants who are delighted to rent the space from you. This section is all about repeating the whole process efficiently and effectively.

We'll explore ways of growing without the growing pains, we'll talk about ways of keeping your WHYs and WHATs (your proposition) relevant and strong, we'll touch on PRODUCTIVITY strategies and, to close this section, we'll talk about COMMUNICATION – a vital part of being able to scale quickly, but also an important part of every aspect of business, and life.

THE GROWTH

One of the things that will take up loads of your time as you grow is recruitment. You want the best people in your team, but not in terms of skills and experience – these are greatly overrated these days. The digital industry moves so quickly that what's relevant now may be obsolete in 12 months. You are looking for people who fit in your organisation and are good at learning. Getting the right people in your team is important, and you will most probably have some of your senior people involved in the interview process, at least at the final stage after the candidates have gone through the first few stages. You'll probably want to meet the candidate yourself before the final decision is made. This takes time but it's the lesser evil. The problem here is that if you keep recruiting junior staff as the direct result of onboarding new clients, you will have to face two big issues at some point:

1. You can't find the people.

2. You run out of space.

You can't find the people: Therefore you hold back on your business development activity because you don't have the resources to deliver. Frustrating! Really freakin' frustrating. Imagine receiving a call from a great brand that wants to work with you but you can't find the resources. Do you outsource and risk your reputation? What do you do?

You run out of space: You have to move office. Moving office can cost tens of thousands and take loads of everyone's time. When there are 5 or 10, even 15 of you, this is not so bad. When you get to 30 or 40, moving office becomes a larger project. Great if you are moving to a new super cool location. Bad when the only reason motivating the move is that you no longer physically fit in the premises. Inevitable at times, but you really ought to avoid doing it unnecessarily.

It pays off to proactively seek solutions before these become real problems. The solution lies in automation and extending the team outside the office. In 2015, Hubshout conducted a survey and found that 58.6 percent of digital agencies were outsourcing SEO to other agencies[1]. The motivation for many of these was probably margin, and they might have been outsourcing to countries where labour is cheaper. Often this means compromising the quality of the work done, which you must avoid at all costs. Easier said than done, but I think there is a solution.

Satelliting

With the growth of coworking spaces like WeWork, Spaces and many others, the possibilities are increasing. Coworking spaces used to be mainly for small teams. Today, they easily accommodate organisations with hundreds of employees. There were very few affordable coworking spaces until just a couple of years ago. Today, they are everywhere, and more are being built all the time. So there are certainly other solutions available.

Satelliting is just one of them – one I like, as it breaks the limitations of a fixed location. Satelliting offers something in the middle, something where you don't have to outsource

---

1 Source: https://www.entrepreneur.com/article/310396

to people on the other side of the world, which might make communication and quality control difficult to manage, but at the same time, you don't have to move office every year as you outgrow the space. This is something we're trying to implement right now – late! But better late than later, and a lot better than too late. Because we have always used our own tech, which requires a very specific methodology, this always seemed harder to do. Now we're making our methodology a lot clearer and rely a lot less on tech that needs to be adapted to the extent it has been in the past. Perhaps now we're also a little bit braver, or more desperate. Probably both.

In practice

Here's how you can do this:

If you have worked out your WHYs, WHATs, OKRs and your people attributes, then this will be much easier. One of the most important things to do when creating a team of people outside of your office is to give them access to your team, your training and the energy, and enable collaboration. To do this you must start with the same mindset you'd have if you were opening real offices around the world. We've opened a small satellite office in Scotland, one in Germany and, as I write this, we're looking in other European locations. Many of the agencies we've talked to about this reported that most of the freelancers they have tried didn't work out. They also reported that the exercise is still worth doing because the benefits of extending the team outside the office can be massive, even if only a few freelancers end up working out.

We wanted to change this by not forming a team of freelancers but rather an extension of our team – a series of satellite offices, a decentralized organisation that doesn't quite match but is closer to Daniel Hulme's idea of a completely decentralised and hierarchies structure. To do this, we needed to turn the recruitment process on its head a little bit, which is fun.

Here are the steps:

Write job description

The job description document you need to show your satellite candidates might be different from the one that you'd use for the same role if it was in-house. It needs to include things about independent working, workload management, travel to the office and other elements that you might not need when you're hiring people who'll be based in the office. You might also need to include items about reporting, virtual meetings and completing training remotely. KPIs must be measurable and clear.

Find freelancers

We are testing PeoplePerHour.com, where you place a brief, people start 'bidding' for the role and off you go. You might receive an overwhelming number of messages, so be prepared. The clearer the brief, the better the whole process and the fewer irrelevant questions you'll have to reply to. Other sites include Upwork, Freelancer, and Hubstaff.

Meetings

When possible, I'd have the new starters spend the first week or so in the office. Then, for the first three months, I'd have them come to the office weekly or monthly, depending on the distance between you. Get them to meet everyone, put them through the training, in person. Going forward, I'd make sure they attend every team meeting, staff update or other event held in the office via Hangout or another video calling system. Whenever possible, have them visit the office.

Paperwork

Be mindful that if you hire freelancers, you might not be able to have them work on certain accounts if your agreement with your customer doesn't allow it. If you've signed an NDA with your customer, the agreement doesn't need to specify that you're not allowed to use third parties; by default you are not allowed. So you'll need to get consent from your customers. You'll also need service agreements. Freelancers will often have these but I'd recommend you write your own – one that includes a solid NDA. And don't forget, the GDPR must be satisfied. Because they work remotely, security of data is paramount. Consult your legal team about this – don't get caught on silly things like this, pay a couple of grand and get the right advice.

Hire them

In the first instance, until you are sure the freelancers you're working with are really good, contract work, either zero-hours or otherwise, might work well. Once you find good people, I'd try to hire them if you can. The idea is to form a team of people who can work remotely, either from home or from a services office, a coworking space, the latter being far more preferable. These people must share your mission, your WHYs. It will take time, but I think it's a worthwhile exercise if you want to grow without being held back by space or lack of talent in your vicinity.

Actions

- At Genie, we've been reactive to this: we addressed it

when the problem arose. Be proactive instead. Draft a document that outlines some ideas of how you can address the challenge of growth.

- Ensure you have clear methodologies, job descriptions and quality control processes to help you with your decentralised office, if this is the route you might take.

- Ensure your mission, your WHY is documented and embedded in all the employee/contractor communication. This will help you keep everyone aligned if you do decide to open satellite offices.

THE REPEAT OF
THE WHYs AND WHATs

There will come a time when you're going to need to reinvent your agency. At the beginning, when you got going, you developed your value proposition, your tone of voice, your branding and your image, and you found your edge. You have defined THE WHY, THE WHAT, THE HOW, THE PEOPLE and everything else we've looked at. You've built it, grown it and you'll realise that you have to repeat the whole process. There will come a time when you have to really shake things up and review everything from top to bottom, from your mission to the critical questions.

At Genie Goals we realised that a few years ago, so we took a mountain trip. We needed a session outside the office, in an environment that was very detached from the office and where we could view the business from a fresh angle. It was Ciaron, Paul, Louis (our Head of R&D), and I, and we questioned everything, because doing things a certain way just because that's how they've always been done isn't a great idea. (Ask Maria's grandma from the previous chapter, she'll tell you.)

We asked ourselves questions like: "If we were to start afresh, what would we do? What would we call the business? What would the mission be?"

We followed a specific methodology from the book Sprint: *How to Solve Big Problems and Test New Ideas in Just Five*

Days by Jake Knapp. The title says it all – the methodology is designed to take an idea from concept to a working prototype in five days. We adapted it slightly – we only had three days, so we did it in three longer days instead of five regular days. I strongly advise you to read the book if you're interested in doing something like that.

In short, for us the three-day session was a process-driven approach that allowed us to almost reinvent our business and to come away with crystal clear priorities, critical questions, a direction and a mission. Our mission came out to be "Revolutionise Digital Marketing for Many Great Retail Brands". Some of our critical questions included things like: "How will we stay ahead of our competitors?" and "How will we keep our customers loving us?"

Our office is based in Cambridge, but we went to Italy to do this – we rented a large, beautiful and very isolated villa at the top of a mountain, near where I grew up. The villa was in the middle of a large estate which was empty at that time of the year – just us in the whole place. With the exception of the 20-minute high-intensity interval training (HIIT) session held each morning in the massive garden, we locked ourselves in for the three days.

One day, the cleaning team came to the house, wanting to clean it. They knocked at the door. I opened the door and their faces all went pale: fear. The house was plastered in Post-Its – they were everywhere, on walls, on the furniture, on doors, anywhere that would take them. We wrote on the windows with markers and stuck pieces of paper anywhere we could. But the cleaning staff's reaction seemed odd, as we would have taken everything off before leaving. One of them said: "Hi, we came to clean". Still confused by their reaction, I mumble something about not needing them to clean because we had to get on with things and we'd be leaving in the next day or two. I mentioned that we were on a tight schedule and that the marker on the windows wasn't permanent, we'd clean it. The terror on their faces seemed to grow stronger. I was very confused. Then they left and we carried on with our session, amused and still unsure as to what had just happened.

After a while it all came together, we finally understood what had caused them to act so terrified. This particular drawing:

What was supposed to look like me on the phone listening to a customer talking about their objectives looked like a crazy dude with spiky hair holding a massive gun, still smoking, and a police negotiator on the phone trying to stop him… me.

Although we wouldn't have been too surprised if the police had visited the estate in the hours that followed, we pressed on. We made progress, and soon, by sticking with the process, the vision became very clear. We had a solid and committed plan with a mission that was full of meaning. Every single piece of the mission statement, every single word, had a profound meaning we all bought into. Every single step of the journey seemed a lot clearer. We knew why we would be doing what we were going to do, and to a great degree, we knew how.

You know, usually you do planning sessions and you leave inspired and pumped, only to forget 90 percent of what made you excited after just a few weeks. This felt different. A bit like the difference between going to see a house you want to buy and actually making the offer.

If you take the time and the courage to do this, I can promise you won't regret it. This is something that we did when we were a team of about 20 people, I think. I don't know if there is a specific size at which it makes more sense to think about doing stuff like this, probably not, but what I do know for sure is that sessions like this are an incredible opportunity to gain clarity, momentum and the unstoppable desire to go after your mission. Do it.

Actions

- Plan a *Sprint*-like session out of the office every year.

- Communicate it to your senior management (or whoever will be involved) and get their buy-in.

- Book it and put it in your diary.

THE PRODUCTIVITY

In order for you to repeat the things you've done that worked and keep growing your agency, you need to get the most out of our time, both in terms of getting shit done and, crucially, feeling good about your working day. Some call this 'productivity'.

Being productive isn't just about getting as much work done as possible. It isn't about grinding through the day and coming out at the end of it screaming "yeah, I've worked my ass off, now I can go home and die!" It's about feeling good about your work. If you finish your day and you feel that you haven't done as much, or as well, as you wanted to, you just don't feel good about yourself. Your confidence gets dented. You feel lethargic and low on energy. And these are not good feelings to have about something you're going to do for a very long time.

There are many elements that may affect your productivity, but I feel that there are three very simple elements that are most likely to produce a remarkable improvement with very little work. I have three tips – three habits to stop, really, which by stopping will allow your productivity to skyrocket and, most importantly, enable you to experience more enjoyment and more happiness at work.

Emails: When you are working on something that you have to get done that day, something important, you should absolutely close your inbox. Unless you are an emergency heart surgeon or someone who might be called in an emergency, you don't need to reply to every email within the hour. That is directly connected and related to the 'fear of missing out', FOMO, which is the intense desire to be up-to-date with whatever might be happening on social media, on your emails and other channels you might be connected to, for the fear of missing out on something. We find it increasingly hard to detach and disconnect from these channels that allow us to 'stay connected' because of this, often subconscious, fear of missing out.

Park your emails in a way that you don't see the notifications. This is because your brain will activate and focus on the email as soon as the notification appears. "What is it? I'm curious and I want to see. No. I'll look at it later. Oh but it might be important". This is the typical thought process that comes to my mind, and this thought process is already at work, it is already messing with us. Flow is already interrupted, even if you decide to ignore the email. Your brain is already fixated on the bloody email, even if you don't know who it is from or what it says. So, park your emails and turn your notifications off. Kill it until you choose to check your emails in a dedicated session. Kill the FOMO.

Multitasking: There is no such thing as multitasking, it's a myth. What we think of as multitasking is really 'part tasking'. You have, let's say, 100 points of attention that you can give to anything. If you're doing one thing, you're doing that one thing with your 100 attention points. The moment you start doing something else at the same time, some of those 100 points must go to that other task. You dedicate some of your attention, whether conscious or unconscious, to the second task and keep some with the first, which means you're not doing either of those things as well as you could.

This isn't an opinion that I'm sharing with you, this is backed by many studies, all with similar results. One such study conducted at the University of Michigan[1] involved asking young adults to switch between tasks such as solving maths problems and identifying geometric objects. The researchers found that whenever participants switched between tasks, it would take time to do so and the amount of time used to switch increased as the complexity of the tasks increased. They observed that whilst switching tasks once doesn't cost much time, when people switch back and forth between different tasks, the amount of time 'wasted' doing so is considerable. The conclusion was that multitasking is indeed inefficient.

The researchers behind the Michigan study came up with a model to explain this: they suggest that when switching tasks, the brain must go through two steps or decisions. The first is called goal shifting, which involves choosing to switch to a new task. The second is called rule activation, where the brain turns off the cognitive rules of the previous task to activate the ones of the new task.

For example, if you have just completed your P&L account for the month and want to shift to preparing a pitch for a new customer, you must first decide that you have completed your P&L (goal shifting) and then turn off the rules that numeric tasks involve to then activate the ones for creating the pitch (rule activation).

In his book *Thinking Fast and Slow*, Daniel Kahneman writes about the brain as two different systems: System 1 and System 2. System 1 takes care of the actions that come super-easily – changing gear for experienced drivers, adding 2+2, etc. System 2 is at work when you change gears the first time you drive, or you need to multiply 124 by 240. When using System 2, there are massive changes at the physiological level – we are forced to slow down to think because we're thinking harder. Even the

---

1 Source: https://www.apa.org/monitor/oct01/multitask.aspx

heart rate increases when System 2 is at work.

Tasks get harder when you work both systems at the same time. If you had to work out 124 x 240 whilst driving (which you should not do), even if you're an experienced driver, your attention would be divided, and you would be distracted, but you'd have a shot at solving it. If you were to try to solve the multiplication whilst parallel parking (which you really should not do), it would be much, much harder, even impossible, to do either of the two tasks.

Don't fall into their trap of believing that you can multitask. Unfortunately for you, you cannot, no one can.

Your phone: If you want to listen to music while you carry out a task, that's excellent, but make sure that your phone is either silenced or that no notifications of any kind come through. Obviously, if you feel that you need to keep the phone so that somebody can call you in an emergency, that's fine. But kill everything else. Notifications are the worst. Even if you don't act on them, a notification popping up makes your brain want to open it. "What is it? Am I missing out on something? Should I check it?" It's horrible, it can consume you.

Make sure that you block periods of time where you are totally undisturbed. You can start with an hour at a time, then two hours, three, and then continue to build up to longer periods, depending on how comfortable you are diving into this. You will see your productivity skyrocket.

These three factors are all interruptions, and interruptions will take you out of flow or prevent you from going into flow. (We talked about the concept of flow earlier in the book; if you don't remember it clearly, go back to it, because it really makes a massive difference. When you work in flow, you get things done more easily and with more enjoyment.)

Two productivity heroes

As well as the three habits which are a good idea to get out of the way, here are a couple of tips on things that you can introduce to become more productive and enjoy your day more.

Post-Its: This is incredibly effective for me and has changed the way I work. The practice of writing down on a Post-It the task, project or part of the project that you want to get done the next day. You have to do this at the end of your day for the following day. You should have a maximum of three Post-Its, with one item on each, and no more.

The idea is that even if you get to the end of the next day and all you've done is the three items on your three Post-Its, that will have been a good day. The flip side is that you must absolutely do all three tasks. Stuff may come up, and at times you may not be able to complete them all, but that has to be the exception. As a rule, you should be able to complete these three items most of the time.

Because you do this exercise the night before, you are more rational about deciding what you're going to do. If you wait until the morning, after you've checked your emails and been inundated by everything that's been thrown at you, you will make that decision way more emotionally, based on who's shouting the loudest and who's pushing your buttons the hardest. If you do it the night before, you are likely to be more strategic about it. The level of satisfaction that you get from taking each Post-It, crunching it up and throwing the little shit in the bin, and getting to the end of the day having completed all that you wanted to is incredible. It's very rewarding. When I start the morning with three Post-Its, I feel determined to get rid of them, and then when I do get rid of them, I feel good.

Location: Try to change location within the office if you can

– change desks or go and work at a standing station, if you have one. Or maybe work from a coffee shop sometimes. You'll find that doing this might increase your productivity and your ability to get into and stay in flow. There are studies showing that every now and again changing the office around increases productivity. By moving around and working from a coffee shop (and if you are in Amsterdam, by coffee shop I mean a café, not one of your coffeeshops), you might find it can have a positive impact on your productivity.

Actions

Close your inbox and notifications when working on projects that don't require them.

- Do one thing at the time. Don't multitask, you can't anyhow.

- Put your phone away, in another room if you can.

- Use Post-Its; write down one task on each Post-It the night before. Stick to three and do them all.

- Work at different locations regularly.

THE COMMUNICATION

We're almost at the at the end. We've covered a massive amount and talked about many elements and subjects, all of which require clear communication between all parties – customers, staff and contacts. By its very nature, this book aims to help you build and grow your agency business to higher levels and to repeat the same process to grow it even more. This implies movement, continuous change, and change is often resisted if communication is suboptimal.

Every year billions of pounds are spent on communication: books, courses, training, coaching, and many other products, all designed to make us better communicators. It's not surprising if you consider that communication is vital in pretty much every one of the concepts we've looked at. I'm not expecting to cover the subject of communication at length here – to do that, you need a specialist, which I am not, and another 75,000 words, which we don't have. However, I have developed expertise in some areas of communication that are specific to building a business:

- Narrative

- Transparency

- Asking questions

- Listening

- Directness

- Smiling

- Weak language

Narrative

If you're delivering the great news that you just won a new customer, but you do it in a way that isn't passionate or enthusiastic, people won't feel as pumped about the new contract as they might if you came in wearing a red cape, jumping on a desk and screaming: "Yay! We did it again!" Okay, maybe that's a bit much, but you get what I mean. When we win new business, I normally send an email to all staff about how great the brand we just won the contract with is, and how we won them. The narrative is more important than the outcome, the vast majority of the time.

Similarly, when you lose a customer, when they leave, the way in which you deliver that news can make all the difference. I'm not talking about pretending or lying, I am suggesting you should tell your staff that you're pleased your customer left. "We lost this contract, and it sucks, but I believe that with our ability and our commitment to becoming the best agency in the world, we are going to go out and find new customers. If we made a mistake with this customer, we will use this as an opportunity to never make the same mistake again, and through this become better." The same goes for when you talk to a customer about poor performance of some campaigns, or a mistake you made on their project. Bad news is bad news; you can sugar-coat it all you like, but it will still be bad news.

The narrative and the passion, the way in which you communicate messages to people, can really make a massive difference to what people are going to do next. When we receive bad news, all we have is what we're going to do about it – all we have is what we're going to do next. The past is gone, we can't change it. The future, however, is affected by our actions, and a good, sincere, and inspiring narrative can have a profound influence on what we, and others, decide to do next.

Transparency

Be totally transparent and honest. Whenever organisations begin to hide the truth or change the facts, perhaps because they believe their staff aren't ready to know whatever it is that's being kept secret, bad things happen. People lose trust. People disengage. People lose passion and stop caring. It's better to be frank. And if there's stuff you can't say, try to find a way to make people understand that you can't share the information, and what the reason is. There aren't, or shouldn't be, many things that need to be kept from staff anyway.

I had the bad tendency of not communicating all the things that were happening, often just because I thought that if things were not agreed or confirmed then there was no point in sharing them with the staff. Wrong. People want to know, and if you think about it, that makes a lot of sense. If they are to buy into the mission, your WHY, then they need to know stuff. I started talking more, sharing more during one-to-one catch-ups and if I'm away, I record video updates telling all staff what we've got going on, even if it's not confirmed. Everyone loves it.

Ask

Ask questions and be quiet. Whenever possible, don't say, ask instead. When doing appraisals, for example, instead of declaring your verdict, ask questions. This is the traditional approach: "Hey John, we're going to talk about your work today. We feel that, in quarter one, you have done well here, you have done really well there, and we feel that you can improve

273

here. For next term we'd love to see you do A and B."

A much better way to go about it would be to ask questions, like: "Hey John, how do you feel you have done in this area?" Let John talk. "Is there anything you feel you needed more support with?" Let him talk... "Is there anything you feel you want to get involved in in the future?" You get the gist. And always strive to find out how 'John' feels on a more personal level and what he wants to do in future. Ask questions like: "How are things?" and, yes you guessed it, let John talk. "What's your North Star? Where do you want to be or what do you want to do in the future?"

That's the difference between managing and coaching.

During one-to-one meetings and regular catch-ups, many managers tend to go through the workload, projects, and to-do lists. If you don't do this already, instead try to sit down, or go for a walk, and ask stuff like "How are you? How are you feeling? What's on your mind? What are you excited by or struggling with? What bugs you? What can I do better to support you?" Ask open questions, and then be quiet. Shut up, really be quiet, and just listen.

Listen

Once we've asked a question, we must listen, truly listen. 90 percent of the time people, especially more junior staff, will say one thing but actually mean something else. They don't do that because they're lying, it's the way humans communicate. Sometimes we don't fully know what we mean or what we really feel until we verbalise it and ask ourselves questions. "I don't feel I'm doing very well here" can sometimes mean "I don't feel I've got the support to do well here", "I don't think I have the tools", or "I don't think I have the time", or it could mean "I don't really give a shit because I don't understand the big WHY, you've not explained it to me". But they won't tell you that unless you ask open questions and then listen carefully. We can then ask 'clarifying questions' that help us offer the best help.

When we listen, we must not listen just with our ears, but also with our eyes. When you pay attention to other things, like body language, you will quickly see if a person is uncomfortable with what they're trying to say, or with what you are saying. You can then adjust your questions and your behaviour accordingly. I have studied communication and body language extensively, mainly through coaching training, leadership and neuro linguistic programming (NLP) training, and the truth is that you don't need any of that to read someone's body language and understand when people are uncomfortable, in disagreement or disengaged. If you listen and observe carefully, you'll know it. You might not know exactly what's bugging them, but you'll know something in their mind has changed.

Then, you can ask direct questions to find out more: "John, I might be reading too much into your body language here and if that's the case, please tell me, but I get the feeling that you might have thoughts about this. It's really important to me that I take all your thoughts on board, so please feel free to say what's on your mind. What are your thoughts or questions about this?" Questions like this can give people the licence to say what's on their mind and help you create a truly open and collaborative team. You were transparent with John about how you felt, you gave him a good narrative and you asked a good question. Now listen.

Listening is probably one of, if not the most important skill in communication and it doesn't come natural to me. But I am getting better. I am working on it and I am much better now than I was a few years ago, and the more I realise I don't know it all, the better I get.

This, in my opinion, is the most important thing of all, the most important concept in this whole book: the concept of getting better, not perfect. If you progress a little every day in whatever you do, if every week you are a little bit better than you were the previous week, you are doing the right thing, better than most. You are growing, making progress, and progression is the secret to happiness. But that's another book – watch this space.

Smile

The world is a beautiful place. Life is short, remember: at the age of 42, statistically speaking, I only have 500 months left, and it's not just me, it's the same for all of us. Months go by quickly. Weeks go by so quickly. Hours go by so quickly. We are here to enjoy life, so let's not take each other too seriously; smile! Say good morning to people you don't know. Look up, don't look down when you walk. Look up and look at people you know and people you don't know and say, "Good morning. I hope you have a great day."

I walk into the office in the morning and I make a point of going around all the banks of desks and saying good morning to everyone, not just the people sitting next to me. I try to smile as much as I can; even though I suck at it naturally, I still try. I try to bring positive energy as much as I can. And I fail plenty – I fail at many things, many times. Communication is one of these. I know how important it is, I trained in it and studied it, and I still fail at it often. But I try, and I get better. I progress, and thus I am happy.

Weak language

"What I mean is...", "Basically...", "Essentially...", "What I'm trying to say..." "I hope you don't mind me saying..."

This is crazy, right? This is called 'weak language' – words and phrases that we put into sentences but that add absolutely zero value to the message we're trying to deliver. The end result is that we send much longer messages, which capture less attention from the people receiving them, because they get bored. Important stuff might be missed. Weak language dilutes the importance of the core message. Here a list of stuff that we typically include in messages which we shouldn't:

- **"As I said before"**: what's the value in telling someone you said something before?

- **"What I mean is…"**: just say what you mean.

- **"If you don't mind"**: you don't know if they mind or not. Just say what you want to say and see if they mind.

- **"Hope this is okay with you"**: as above.

- **"I just wanted to…"**: just do it.

- **"Basically"**: what does 'basically' even mean?

- **"To keep it short"**: just keep it short.

- **"Literally", "Kind of "**: zero value.

- **"The way I see it"**: just say the way you see it.

- **"I might be wrong"**: if you are wrong, saying that you might be wrong won't help you.

- **"Pretty much"**: what is this?

And, before you judge me, before you go on to say: "there's

weak language in your book, Luca", I am talking about direct, transactional communication here – messages and conversations, mainly in business. I always try to eliminate weak language, but there are times when we might choose to use it to give stuff colour, like I do sometimes in this book. There are times when I include weak language simply because I forget to cut it out, because I make mistakes, like everyone else does, even in the field we're 'experts' in. The point is to be aware of it and strive to always refine and improve. Get better.

For professional emails, especially when you want something from someone, make sure you clear your message of all weak language. Here's an example, an excerpt of a real-life email I received from someone – I've edited out the weak language that appeared in the original:

"Hi Luca,

The XXXXX ~~Event had lots of new sponsors confirmed recently and we are now up to 16.~~

~~This means~~ I only have a few packages remaining so I wondered if you would be interested in a "Proof of Concept" roundtable ~~package~~? (which is ~~basically a heavily discounted package that we use to prove how good the event is in the hope it will allow us to establish a long-term relationship with you guys~~)."

Here's a breakdown of what I cut:

- **"Event had lots of new sponsors confirmed recently and we are now up to 16"**: Who cares? She has already said that they only have a few packages remaining, which implies they sold a lot.

- **"Package"**: adds no value, it's implied.

- **"Basically"**: you know why I took this out.

- **"that we use to prove how good the event is in the hope it will allow us to establish a long-term relationship with you guys)"**: just needs to say that they are discounting the package to prove the quality, which can be said in fewer words. The fact that they want to prove how good the event is so we buy again is implied.

This is what the new version looks like:

"Hi Luca,
   I only have a few packages remaining for the XXXXX event. Would you be interested in a "Proof of Concept" roundtable heavily discounted to prove to you how good the event is?"

From 76 words to 34 and it says the same thing, only much better. The whole email was about 230 words. Imagine the impact clearing the message of weak language could have on its effectiveness.

   This is a great example of how we can increase the effectiveness of our communication just by getting rid of some words. Less is more.

   "If you can't explain it simply you don't understand it well enough"
   – Albert Einstein.

Be concise

Write short messages. Long messages are intimidating, because everyone is busy and no one has the time to read them. Even if something caught the reader's attention at the start of the message, they are more likely to put it off and 'read it later' (which often means they'll never read it). Also, being able to say what you want to say in an email very concisely is a sign that you're smart and respect the recipient's time. The way I approach this is to write the first draft and then read it with the mission to take out two elements:

- **Weak Language:** you know all about that. :)

- **Repetition:** It can be tempting to repeat something – a point we really want to make, something that is super important. We do this because that's how we speak. When we talk to someone, we want to make sure they hear and understand the important parts and so we repeat ourselves. But in writing, this really doesn't work. If you think about it, it makes little sense, but most do it anyway. The message in an email is written down, it won't disappear once it's been read, so it can be seen and reread as many times as the recipient wants. If something is important, you should just make sure that it comes across as such and perhaps isolate it in a dedicated paragraph instead of embedding it in a large one.

Like this one here!

Being concise is very effective in communicating clearly and is also a sign of respect for the person you're writing to.

"I didn't have time to write a short letter, so I wrote a long one instead" – Mark Twain

Actions

- Use the narrative: Give context, tell the story. Try incorporating the narrative in your communication as

280

much as you can from now on.

- Be transparent: Say all you can to your teams and customers, they are your family at work.

- Ask questions: Coaching is better than managing. Ask open questions about the person and their feelings. To do lists can be discussed in dedicated business meetings.

- Listen: Really listen with ears and eyes.

- Smile: As much as you can.

- Weak language: Cut it out.

- Keep it short: Respect their time, be concise.

THE END

Thursday night, 19th of July 2001. Just landed at Stansted Airport. I make it to Cambridge with £65 in my pocket. My first week's rent is £95. I'm already £30 in debt and have not even fully arrived yet. A friend who's been in Cambridge for some years introduces me to a half Italian lady who runs a temp agency. She sends me to Loch Fyne, a fish restaurant in town, to wash dishes.

That was a day after I landed. I couldn't speak a word of English. Nothing. When people spoke to me it just sounded like garbled noise. Like in the movie *Bruce Almighty*, when Bruce casts a spell on Evan that prevents him from speaking properly while he's doing a live news broadcast: "Rahrahrahrahrahrahrah Rahrahrahrahrahrahrah".

At Loch Fyne, they'd ask me to do stuff and I'd look at them trying to guess from their body language whether I was moving in the right direction. At the end of the first shift they told me to go home. I thought they were saying: "Go home, you're tired, you worked very hard. Go home and rest". What they were actually saying to me, it turned out, was: "Go home, never come back. You cannot work here".

But the lady at the agency took me under her wing. She liked me in a motherly kind of way, so she sends me to the beautiful Cambridge Colleges to do silver service. Doing silver service you don't have to talk to anyone, you just follow every other waiter and do what they do. You pick up a tray and go around the long tables of students and put food on their plates.

Eventually, my English got good enough that I could become a proper waiter. That was a massive milestone. I left Italy as a marketing manager at the age of 25 and found myself in a country where I couldn't communicate, even at the most basic level. I got fired from a kitchen porter role. Becoming a waiter at that point felt like I was becoming the MD of Tesla. A bit of a Marmite type analogy, I know.

Eventually I become the Manager, then the Managing Director and shareholder of a small chain of restaurants in Cambridge. The flagship unit was CB2 Bistro. I brought some marketing buzz to it and we doubled our revenue in one year, and built an outside area, which went on to win a design award. It was a copy of an Italian piazza in Marostica, Northern Italy, which has a human-sized chess board in the middle. We built a place everyone loved, customers and staff. We had a list of people wanting to work there. It felt like family.

One day this South African girl came in. She was beautiful. The most beautiful girl I had ever seen. She had a relaxed, confident "I don't take life too seriously" kind of look on her face. The kind of look of somebody who is comfortable in herself but not arrogant. Just comfortable. She came up to the counter to order a coffee. I said: "where are you from?" "I'm from South Africa" she said, probably thinking: "there you go, another guy trying to make up some cheap talk, how do I shake him?" (She didn't think that :) .) "What's your name?", I asked. "Karen. Yours?" She grabbed her coffee and went back to her table where her friends were sitting, and that was it, I'd fallen in love. I just didn't know it yet.

During that time I was considering a move to San Francisco, where I could get closer to the tech startup world that interested me. As crazy as it sounds, I decided to put the San Francisco trip on hold. I don't know why, it felt like the right thing to do.

I wanted to get to know Karen, I wanted to ask her out. But every time she came in, she was always in a group. I could never quite tell whether she had a boyfriend. I became frustrated, so I made a promise to myself: "the next time she comes in, irrespective of whether she is alone or with fifty friends, I will ask her out". I don't know about you, but when I make a promise or throw a challenge to myself, I just can't back off. If I'm working out and I have the thought "I bet you can't do ten more", then I'm gonna have to do it.

One evening Karen came in, it was the first time that she wasn't in a large group. Instead, she was with three other people – one woman and two men. It was the worst possible scenario, a double date. Damn. "But I promised! I have to do it." So at the end of the night, after procrastinating for hours, I approached the table and said: "Hey, do you like jazz? Do you like jazz music?" "Yes", she said. "There's a live jazz night on at La Raza in town on Wednesday, do you want to go?" I asked. "Yes". Tongue in cheek, I replied: "But that's a date!" "Yep, that's cool", she said. The guy sitting next to her looked at me and said: "What that hell... I've been trying with her for three months, man!"

Time went by, my English got better and so I was able to open a small marketing consultancy, which led to a small graphic design agency. I liked hustling so I also opened an Italian, South African and French Deli, a personal development coaching business and a complementary health centre. In the meantime, I met an incredible number of people, some of whom became good friends.

One of these people was Ciaron, the MD of Genie Ventures. I met Ciaron at CB2 when he came in with his family for dinner. I ended up being his lodger for a year or so. A few years after we met, Ciaron called me to say they had developed a great piece of tech to manage media buying for one of their comparison websites. They wanted to take it to market as an agency proposition, and he wanted to pick my brains as to how they might do that. The very fact that he asked me made me – and still makes me – very proud. We had a conversation and we went on with our lives.

A couple of years later, they were still focusing mainly on the comparison websites, what we refer to as the Publishing Business at Genie Ventures, as the sites were successful and took up most of their time. They then decided to advertise for a business development manager to grow the agency proposition. Something told me that I should reach out to Ciaron. He was a friend and I had the utmost respect for him as a person, despite his passion for watching cricket three days in a row, sitting in the same spot of the sofa and, worst of all, looking as if he was enjoying it.

We ended up deciding that we'd work together. I was going to take the agency to market and attempt to build it and grow it. My goal was big. My first ever cold call was to Groupon. I was ambitious, which meant this project required all my attention. I sold my two businesses and that was the beginning of Genie Goals as we know it today.

Remember Karen? The South African woman I met at CB2? We have now been married for 12 years and we have three beautiful boys. I still feel for her the way I felt when she walked into CB2.

I'm telling you this story is because if you put yourself in the shoes of that Italian guy who, at the age of 25, decided to move to Cambridge with no language skills and no money, you'd see the odds were against you. The odds that you would go on to give tens of talks to large audiences, in English, some on behalf of Google, build eight businesses, including a top 3 percent

Google ranked, multi-award-winning digital agency, be ranked a top five international marketing expert and be married to a South African woman for more than 12 years, would be very, very small.

Most people wouldn't put their money on it.

I am not bragging for the sake of bragging. I've fucked up in life too, like most people... probably more than most. I am more than happy to tell you all the stuff I've done wrong, the mistakes I've made and the stuff I regret. Seriously, you fancy that? Give me a call, but bring the beers and a sleeping bag, because it's going to take a while. And you can write it all down and put it online if you want. I am serious, I know I'm not perfect. And that's the point of this closing chapter.

If ADHD diagnoses had been in fashion when I was younger, I'd have been given one. Ms Gandini really believed I was not going to do anything with my life. She saw it in her self-made mental crystal ball: in it, I was a criminal or a drug addict at worst, and a lazy parasite at best.

I was the Christmas toy that comes broken in the box, that has to be fixed before it can be used. I was an outcast, an overweight, lazy-eyed boy from a family that was different from most around us, for all the wrong reasons. I couldn't study past the age of 13. At the age of 25, I found myself in a new country, unable to communicate at the most basic level, with no money, no friends and no family, and I managed to get fired from washing dishes in a restaurant. I did what I did from a position of disadvantage.

What I've achieved is nothing compared to what some people do. There are some truly remarkable individuals who create innovations and radically change the course of our planet. Volunteers in disaster zones. Medics and emergency response workers who protect us and save lives. Teachers and carers who help us raise the people of the future. These are heroes. Hats off and thank you to those people.

What I've done is nothing like that, but I have managed to build and grow remarkable businesses and positively impact hundreds, if not thousands, of people in the process. I have the amazing opportunity to touch people in a positive way. When I receive emails to tell me that something I did inspired someone to do something they thought they couldn't, I feel alive. Truly alive.

So yes, I've done some good work, and if I've done this much with not having much to do it with, then absolutely anyone can BUILD, GROW and REPEAT whatever they want.

Get your limiting beliefs out of the way. If it's humanly possible, if anyone else can do something, then you can do it too.

How does this relate to you building an agency? It's exactly the same thing. When we started Genie Goals, we did so in a cluttered marketplace with many large agencies, much bigger than we were. I don't focus on competitors. I don't look at them. I don't care what they do because I want to do something remarkably different. To me, they were not our competitors.

Instead, I looked at an agency in a different sector. An agency that I looked up to a lot for the way they presented themselves, their passion for the industry as a whole, how they treated their staff and, of course, for their success too. They were called SEOgadget. Today they are called BuiltVisible. Today we are of a similar size to BuiltVisible, and I still look up to them for how they conduct themselves. We share many values.

When we started, Genie Goals could have been compared to that young kid from Italy, and BuiltVisible was one of the role models we had chosen. Today we have many role models – there are many organisations we look up to and get inspired by, including Google.

But the biggest inspiration comes from our most important role model, the Genie Goals of the future. From our staff who believe in our WHYs and shape our WHATs.

It would have been so much easier for me to say: "I'm not going to go to the UK. I'm not going to try this. I can't speak their language". To take the path of least resistance. If I'd done that, if I had taken that path, I'd never have made it to where I am today. It would have been easier for Genie Goals to say: "Let's not be different, let's bring in all sorts of customers, not just the ones we like. Let's make as much profit as possible instead of investing". If we'd done that, we'd never be here, and this book would not exist.

There were many moments when I considered giving up.

The first time I had to go buy bedding for my flat. I went to the shop and I asked: "Can I have two *bad shits*" (not a typo) with the number two formed with my index and middle finger and the back of my hand facing the shop assistant. In short, I told the shop attendant to go fuck herself. She looked at me with a very shocked face and I didn't understand why. I didn't know I was swearing badly at the poor lady. She quickly understood it was unintentional, a language barrier-induced Tourette's of sorts.

One time I was waiting for a friend at a bar. I saw a group of pretty women sitting round a table in the dining area celebrating something. One of them came up to me and said: "teen ton three tom mihe ricks otl like it?" I thought about it for a moment and then said: "Yes". She turned around and went back to the table; I'll never know what she said.

It took me one month to read one page of a book!

There were times when it was hard, horrible and discouraging.

Building an agency, or any business, might feel a bit like this at times. But you have to keep going. Capture the moments of happiness and success and build a solid plan, using all the tools, strategies and tactics you learnt to grow that confidence and know that the challenging times will pass.

Know that you are learning with every adversity you face. What once seemed unattainable will become reality and you'll be able to repeat the process with much less pain. BUILD, GROW and REPEAT.

Whatever you choose, I deeply hope that you will BUILD, GROW and REPEAT your success, in business and life.

And who knows, you might meet the woman or man of your dreams in the process.

Luca Senatore

The End.

THE GRATITUDE

This book would never have been possible without the incredible help of some truly amazing people. If I was to name everyone who contributed to me being able to write this book, I would have to go on for several pages.

But before I dive into naming the people I owe my thanks to specifically for his book, let's briefly look at what giving thanks actually means, and what being truly, deeply grateful does to people.

We are so busy living our lives, facing our challenges, that we often forget to stop and be truly, powerfully, and deeply grateful for all the things that we do have, for all the things that we take for granted, but we absolutely shouldn't.

If you think about it, and if you do some research, you realise that you are in a very, very fortunate position. You are in the very small minority of people who can afford to do the things that you do. According to Giving What We Can[1] and their How Rich Am I tool[2], if you have a combined household income of £60K and have two children, you are in the richest 3.8 percent of the world's population.

Yes, this might take developing countries into account, but we don't have to go that far to see that we're extremely lucky – we see many much less fortunate people on our own streets. Homeless people are everywhere and, whilst it's easy to think that "it's their choice", "they choose to drink their lives away",

1 www.givingwhatwecan.org
2 https://www.givingwhatwecan.org/get-involved/how-rich-am-i/

or "they choose not to work", many of these men and women actually found themselves in these situations before they even realised they were heading there. If you stop and talk to people living on the street, you find that some of them have stories that are absolutely devastating, and that could happen to anyone, even you.

I was on a drunken night out with my friend Massimo a few weeks ago, and as he was busy ordering a burger from the van, I got chatting to a homeless guy. "What happened to you? Why are you on the streets?" I asked. He went on to tell me that his family – his wife and two kids – had left after he lost his job. The going got really tough, they got into frequent and hard arguments and at one point his wife couldn't cope with the situation anymore. She took the two kids and left the country. 'John' looked at me and said: "I didn't know what to do, I started drinking. It seemed like the only place where I could find peace, where I could find silence. And then, before I realised it, I wasn't able to come out of it. Lost my job, lost my house, I lost the will."

It's the same with health. You don't have to go far to see people who have lost their limbs or mobility in accidents. Some of these people go on to do amazing stuff that many 'healthy' people will never do:

- Stephen Hawking, who had Amyotrophic Lateral Sclerosis (ALS), did most of his remarkable work whilst affected by the condition.

- John Nash, who had Schizophrenia from just after college, went on to become one of the most renowned mathematicians.

- Kyle Maynard, born without any arms or legs, went on

to become an award-winning mixed martial arts athlete, climbed Mount Kilimanjaro without prosthetics, is a member of the National Wrestling Hall of Fame, and is a motivational speaker for the Washington Speaker's Bureau.

There are many more people who have done amazing things with physical, psychological, or circumstantial disadvantages. Most of them are not in the public eye, but they exist. It's not just the few famous ones. These people pushed through pain and hardship that to most of us is unimaginable. But they didn't complain, they took charge. You don't achieve things like that without taking charge.

Yet, sometimes we let arguments with our friends, with our partners, with our clients, affect our mood for days, even weeks. We let a punctured tyre upset our mood. The man who cuts us off on the road, the little scratch on the new car, the internet not working. We let these things drag us down, take our happiness and energy. We let these events affect us and those around us. Fuck those petty little hurdles, we will overcome them.

Put things into perspective and these things have little or no power over us.

Sometimes I stop and think: "What if I get a phone call and my wife tells me that one of our kids in severely injured? What if the police call me and tell me that they were all in a fatal accident?" My fingers are shaking even as I type this shit! I rarely think about things like this, but it's when I catch myself being pathetic, complaining about petty things. Then I open my eyes, and I know that I'm not in that situation. And it's bliss. Just like when you wake up from a horrible dream and realise it was just a dream. This is what I call perspective.

We must take time out to feel grateful for what we have

today, we might not always have it.

I have this routine which I do 90 percent of the time. When I go to bed, I take five minutes to think of all the things that I'm grateful for. I don't just think about them, I try to feel the feelings these things give me. I think about anything, like being able to feel my wife's shoulder, her skin on my skin when we lie in bed, how lucky I am that I have this person that I admire, respect, and love right there next to me. Not everyone does. It isn't guaranteed. I am not entitled to it.

I think about the beautiful kids that we have, the fact that they are healthy. I think of the fact that, perhaps partly down to luck and genes, but largely down to hard work, I am a decent father to them, able to teach and love them. Not everyone can be a good father. It's not guaranteed. We're not entitled to it.

I touch the mattress and I give thanks for the fact that I can afford to have that under my body, and a roof over my head. Many do not have these, they are sleeping on the streets as I think those thoughts. I thank the people in my life, I am grateful for them all, even the Gandinis and the 'my fathers' of the world, because they have shaped me, opened the door to the next level.

My biggest invitation to you is to be grateful. I really mean it, be grateful for the things that you have, for the coffee that you drink in the morning, the legs that carry you, the lungs that breathe and all that you have. Because you know what? Not everyone has those things, they are not guaranteed, you are not entitled to them, and they might not always be there.

Acknowledgements

For this particular project, the book, I want to thank a few specific people.

First and foremost, I want to thank my wife Karen. By

now you know the circumstances in which Karen and I met even better than my mother does. Karen always puts up with my crazy ideas, including competing in Mixed Martial Arts, supporting me through the weight cuts, the intense training and the extreme psychological places that fighting can take you, and your family, to. She was there. My fights were her fights too.

Her tone of relief when we spoke after a fight, especially when I lost. I could tell in her voice she was relieved that I was in one piece, and when I lost, you could almost detect the hope that since I had lost, maybe now I would retire. And even with all the money, our money, that I risked building businesses, she's always been there like a solid pillar supporting me.

Next, I want to thank Ciaron, because this is us, a team. Genie Goals is the result of our attitude to business, our openness to taking risks, and our commitment to not doing stuff just because we get paid but because we believe these are the right things to do.

Our bullish and aggressive attitude to risk and our commitment to doing stuff that is different and remarkable makes all of this possible and worth doing. We've crashed many times and we will crash again. But I know it will be exciting and fun, and we'll always come out the other side better than we started.

I want to thank Tom, Head of Agency at Genie. Tom's been there from day one, and I can't help but think of him as a younger brother. The changes, evolution, progression that that guy has made in a relatively short period of time are beyond imagination. I can't even begin to describe how good Tom is at understanding concepts, which until a moment before were alien to him, going away and quietly working things out to then come back with a better iteration of what you've done.

His never-ending can-do attitude, ability to stand his ground when he doesn't believe something is right, but also his ability to adopt new methodologies and take risks is commendable. Thank you Tom.

Everyone else on the team. Genie is us, collectively. Thank you for doing what you do every single day. You make coming to work every day a real pleasure.

My mentor, Rob Moore, who has helped me with this book project from the beginning. I had no clue where to start. Rob helped me understand how to plan, structure, and keep the project on track. Thanks to Rob, I wrote this book in just over four months, start to finish. Thanks Rob.

I want to thank all the beta readers, Ciaron, Geoff, Natasha, Alberto and Jenn. You took time to not only read the manuscript, unedited, with all the typos, but to provide feedback that made this book so much better, so much more valuable for the readers. Thank you, thank you, thank you.

Last, but certainly not least, thank you for reading this book. This book is at the edge, and I have absolutely no idea whether you're thinking: "What the hell have I just read?" or "This book's going to change my life", or both, or anything in between. But I know that this book is full of stuff that can change your business, and if you let it, it can add value to your life in general.

Thank you very much for taking the time to read it. If you liked it, please review in on Amazon so more people can find it.

I humbly, humbly, humbly thank you very much. Have a fantastic, amazing, fucking rocking life.

I love you all. The End (really :))

PS: I'd be really grateful if you could spare one minute to leave me your review. Thank you.

Also, remember to connect with me on social media.

THE TOOLS

A few resources and tools I like, in alphabetical order.

Alerts (by Google)

- Monitor the web for new content as it goes live.

- https://www.google.com/alerts

Asana

- Organize and plan workflows, projects, and more.

- https://asana.com

Boomerang for Gmail

- Boomerang adds scheduled sending and email reminders to Gmail, helping you reach Inbox Zero.

- https://www.boomeranggmail.com

G Suite

- An integrated suite of secure, cloud-native collaboration and productivity apps powered by Google AI. Includes Gmail, Docs, Drive, Calendar, Meet and more.

- https://gsuite.google.com

Grammarly

- Writing app to improve quality of writing.

- https://www.grammarly.com

HadBrake

- An open-source, GPL-licensed, multiplatform, multithreaded video transcoder.

- https://handbrake.fr

Hootsuite

- Social media management. Manage different platforms and channels from one place, schedule posts and monitor activity.

- https://hootsuite.com/en-gb

Keyword Tool

- Alternative to Google Ads Keyword Planner for SEO and PPC keyword research across different platforms.

- https://keywordtool.io

LinMailPro

- LinkedIn marketing automation. LinkedIn doesn't like extensions. You should use this tool at your discretion and if you do, do not spam. I'd only automate stuff that you can do as well and as genuinely as you would manually, but in less time.

- https://www.linmailpro.com

Mail Chimp

- Email marketing platform.
- https://mailchimp.com

People Per Hour

- Post a project for free to find professional freelancers of any sort, from VAs to sales, design and more.
- https://www.peopleperhour.com

Rev.com

- Transcriptions, subtitles, captions and more. They rely on a network of hand-picked freelancers. Using technology to offer unbeatable quality, speed, and value.
- https://www.rev.com

Slack

- Cloud-based team collaboration tools.
- https://slack.com

Toggle

- Time tracking app for agencies, teams and small businesses. A simple time tracker with powerful reports and cross-platform functionalities.
- https://toggl.com

99 Designs

- A large number of freelance designers bidding to work on most creative projects.

- https://99designs.co.uk

Made in the USA
Middletown, DE
16 January 2020